CW01433345

Neurodiversity, Faith Formation, and Theological Education

This book demonstrates the constructive insights the neurodiversity paradigm presents for a more thorough understanding of creation, human flourishing, Christian virtues, ecclesiology, belonging, youth ministry, prayer, worship, and justice.

The neurodiversity movement is a social justice movement that celebrates the unique insights and strengths of Autistic people, people with ADHD, learning differences, and other experiences like Tourette's and tics. Rather than viewing such experiences as deficits, the movement emphasizes the natural variation in the ways people think, learn, and live in the world. Yet, people with these diagnoses, who often identify as neurodivergent, have experienced prejudice and stigma in educational and church spaces due to their neurological or behavioral differences. Participation in church and learning environments is often a burden for neurodivergent people. What can theological educators and ministry leaders learn from the neurodiversity paradigm and movement? How might places of learning and worship be transformed by listening to the voices of neurodivergent people?

Drawing on empirical research and lived experience, the contributions to this book pursue answers to these questions and present a vision of faith formation and theological education that centers the voices of neurodivergent people and cultivates environments where people of all neurotypes can flourish. This book was originally published as a special issue of the *Journal of Disability & Religion*.

Michael Paul Cartledge is a practical theologian at Princeton Theological Seminary and teaches courses on neurodiversity, mental health, youth ministry, and Christian education.

Erin Raffety is a cultural anthropologist, a Presbyterian pastor, and an ethnographic researcher who has studied foster families in China, Christian congregations in the United States, and people with disabilities around the world. Raffety teaches and researches at Princeton Theological Seminary and Princeton University, USA.

Neurodiversity, Faith Formation, and Theological Education

Edited by
Michael Paul Cartledge and Erin Raffety

Routledge
Taylor & Francis Group

LONDON AND NEW YORK

First published 2025
by Routledge
4 Park Square, Milton Park, Abingdon, Oxon, OX14 4RN

and by Routledge
605 Third Avenue, New York, NY 10158

Routledge is an imprint of the Taylor & Francis Group, an informa business

Introduction, Chapters 1, 2, 4 and 6–8 © 2025 Taylor & Francis
Chapter 3 © 2023 Krysia Emily Waldock. Originally published as Open Access.
Chapter 5 © 2023 Armand Léon van Ommen, Henna J. Cundill, Krysia Emily Waldock, Catherine Tryfona, Grant Macaskill, Christopher Barber, Sarah Douglas, Bryan W. Fowler, Harry Gibbins, Ian Lasch and Brian Brock. Originally published as Open Access.

With the exception of Chapters 3 and 5, no part of this book may be reprinted or reproduced or utilised in any form or by any electronic, mechanical, or other means, now known or hereafter invented, including photocopying and recording, or in any information storage or retrieval system, without permission in writing from the publishers. For details on the rights for Chapters 3 and 5, please see the chapters' Open Access footnotes.

Trademark notice: Product or corporate names may be trademarks or registered trademarks, and are used only for identification and explanation without intent to infringe.

British Library Cataloguing in Publication Data
A catalogue record for this book is available from the British Library

ISBN13: 978-1-041-02334-0 (hbk)
ISBN13: 978-1-041-02336-4 (pbk)
ISBN13: 978-1-003-61880-5 (ebk)

DOI: 10.4324/9781003618805

Typeset in Minion Pro
by codeMantra

Publisher's Note
The publisher accepts responsibility for any inconsistencies that may have arisen during the conversion of this book from journal articles to book chapters, namely the inclusion of journal terminology.

Disclaimer
Every effort has been made to contact copyright holders for their permission to reprint material in this book. The publishers would be grateful to hear from any copyright holder who is not here acknowledged and will undertake to rectify any errors or omissions in future editions of this book.

Contents

Citation Information

The chapters in this book were originally published in the *Journal of Disability & Religion*, volume 27, issue 4 (2023). When citing this material, please use the original page numbering for each article, as follows:

Introduction
Introduction: Centering Neurodiversity in Theological Education
Michael Paul Cartledge and Erin Raffety
Journal of Disability & Religion, volume 27, issue 4 (2023), pp. 487–490

Chapter 1
Theological Education with Neurodiversity in Mind: Research Insights and Future Possibilities
Michael Paul Cartledge and Erin Raffety
Journal of Disability & Religion, volume 27, issue 4 (2023), pp. 606–619

Chapter 2
Speaking with Us, Not for Us: Neurodiversity, Theology and Justice
Naomi Lawson Jacobs
Journal of Disability & Religion, volume 27, issue 4 (2023), pp. 584–605

Chapter 3
The Impossible Subject: Belonging as a Neurodivergent in Congregations
Krysia Emily Waldock
Journal of Disability & Religion, volume 27, issue 4 (2023), pp. 568–583

Chapter 4
Peculiar Theological Education
Claire Williams
Journal of Disability & Religion, volume 27, issue 4 (2023), pp. 552–567

Chapter 5
United by Neurodiversity: Postgraduate Research in a Neurodiverse Context
Armand Léon van Ommen, Henna J. Cundill, Krysia Emily Waldock, Catherine Tryfona, Grant Macaskill, Christopher Barber, Sarah Douglas, Bryan W. Fowler, Harry Gibbins, Ian Lasch and Brian Brock
Journal of Disability & Religion, volume 27, issue 4 (2023), pp. 537–551

Chapter 6

"Misfitting" and Friendship in the Virtuous Life: Neurodiversity and Moral Formation
Elizabeth Agnew Cochran
Journal of Disability & Religion, volume 27, issue 4 (2023), pp. 491–507

Chapter 7

Dismantling the Supercrip Prof: Theological Education and Faculty Accessibility
Natalie Wigg-Stevenson
Journal of Disability & Religion, volume 27, issue 4 (2023), pp. 520–536

Chapter 8

Disability and Youth Ministry: The Book I'm Not Going to Write
Benjamin T. Conner
Journal of Disability & Religion, volume 27, issue 4 (2023), pp. 508–519

For any permission-related enquiries please visit:
http://www.tandfonline.com/page/help/permissions

Notes on Contributors

Christopher Barber, Department of Divinity, Centre for Autism and Theology, University of Aberdeen, UK.

Brian Brock, Department of Divinity, Centre for Autism and Theology, University of Aberdeen, UK.

Michael Paul Cartledge, Institute for Youth Ministry, Princeton Theological Seminary, USA.

Elizabeth Agnew Cochran, Duquesne University, Pittsburgh, USA.

Benjamin T. Conner, Western Theological Seminary, Holland, USA.

Henna J. Cundilla, Department of Divinity, Centre for Autism and Theology, University of Aberdeen, UK.

Sarah Douglas, Department of Divinity, Centre for Autism and Theology, University of Aberdeen, UK.

Bryan W. Fowler, Department of Divinity, Centre for Autism and Theology, University of Aberdeen, UK.

Harry Gibbins, Department of Divinity, Centre for Autism and Theology, University of Aberdeen, UK.

Naomi Lawson Jacobs, Bantry Bridge Research and Training, Berkshire, UK.

Ian Lasch, Department of Divinity, Centre for Autism and Theology, University of Aberdeen, UK.

Grant Macaskill, Department of Divinity, Centre for Autism and Theology, University of Aberdeen, UK.

Armand Léon van Ommen, Department of Divinity, Centre for Autism and Theology, University of Aberdeen, UK.

Erin Raffety, Institute for Youth Ministry, Princeton Theological Seminary, USA.

Catherine Tryfona, Cardiff School of Technologies, Cardiff Metropolitan University, UK.

Krysia Emily Waldock, Tizard Centre, University of Kent, Canterbury, UK.

Natalie Wigg-Stevenson, Emmanuel College, University of Toronto, Canada.

Claire Williams, Regents Theological College, Worcestershire, UK.

Introduction: Centering Neurodiversity in Theological Education

Michael Paul Cartledge and Erin Raffety

We are pleased to offer the first special issue on "Neurodiversity and Theological Education" in the *Journal of Disability & Religion*, featuring eight original articles from neurodiverse scholars, the majority of which center neurodivergent perspectives in research, scholarship, ministry, and theological education. This centering is significant given the prejudice and stigma autistic people, people with ADHD, dyslexia, dyspraxia, dyscalculia, dysgraphia, Tourette's and tics, have experienced in educational and church spaces due to their neurological or behavioral differences, as well as the relative newness of the term and the movement of neurodiversity, especially when it comes to Christian formation.

Simply put, neurodiversity is the reality that we all think, learn, experience the world, and connect with others in various ways. Although such an assertion may seem commonplace or even basic, the neurodiversity paradigm stands in radical contrast to the pathology paradigm, or the often medicalized presumption that people with such neurological differences are flawed, in need of fixing, or abnormal. It also stands in contrast to the normalizing of certain ways of learning and thinking that implicitly marginalize persons who are "neurominorities" or "neurodivergent," or who do not conform to cultural, educational, or medical standards. Instead, following Nick Walker, a neurodivergent author, educator, and psychologist, a neurodiversity paradigm affirms at least three fundamental principles: (1) neurodiversity affirms natural human variation; (2) there is no single right way of thinking or learning; and (3) the emphasis on diversity in the term highlights dynamics similar to experiences of gender or ethnicity, clarifying that neurodiversity is not just about minds but about power and social experiences (Walker, 2021). It is also important to note that the Neurodiversity Movement, which grew out of the Autism Rights Movement in the 1990s, is a grassroots movement that emerged from communities of neurodivergent thinkers and activists.

The growing field of Theology of Disability acknowledges similar biases against neurodivergent people in churches and seminaries, yet has only recently begun to consider the contributions of neurominorities to theology and theological education, especially on their own terms. However, by centering neurodiversity, this collection demonstrates the constructive insights the neurodiversity presents for a more thorough understanding of creation, human flourishing, Christian virtues, ecclesiology, belonging, youth ministry, prayer, worship, and justice, just to name a few. Centering neurodiversity also uses the language of self-advocates and neurodivergent researchers in a way that emphasizes both the limits and the potential for scholarship and practice.

This is why many of the authors in this collection emphasize their experiences and call for greater methodological transparency in theological knowledge-making. As they construct theology, they illuminate the process of that research, including how data is gathered and who gets to speak and why, because too often those methods have been obscured and neu-rodivergent people have been research objects, even research subjects, but rarely researchers (let alone theologians) themselves. Many of the authors have named, following Miranda Fricker's work, this as epistemic injustice, the inability of neurodivergent people to tell their own stories (2007). In their articles, "Speaking with Us, Not For Us: Neurodiversity, Theology, and Justice" and "The Impossible Subject: Belonging as a Neurodivergent in Congregations," scholars Naomi Lawson Jacobs and Krysia Waldock exemplify the rigor and import of autoethnography as a vital tool toward furthering testimonial justice for neurodivergent people. Waldock illustrates how felt and enacted stigma in Christian congregations create an impos-sible bind for neurodivergent people to conform in Christian congregations in order to belong. As Jacobs so clearly puts it, "The concept of neuro-diversity gives us the tools to challenge our marginalization" (p. 589). As social researchers, Jacobs and Waldock, demonstrate that careful, trans-parent research methods are essential in avoiding merely reproducing the unjust conditions in which neurodivergent people find themselves in con-gregations, the academy, and society.

Because this collection is focused on theological education, many of the articles explore how learning environments, such as seminary class-rooms, post-graduate research, and even faculty accommodations processes can be adapted to provide increased access for neurodiverse learners. In her article on "Peculiar Theological Education," Claire Williams draws on the neurodiversity paradigm to reclaim the word "peculiar" as a rich and specific contribution from autistic theologians. Drawing on black, womanist, and liberation theologians, Williams conjures post-Pentecostal classrooms where autistic teachers and learners resist conformity through a plurality of communication and through conscientization that disrupts theological curriculum by reckoning with its history of oppression. Reflecting on their experiences as a neurodiverse community of learners, postgraduates from the Center for Autism and Theology identify the ways in which their affirmational theology and "eclectic" communication challenges the status quo by centering autistic perspectives in research and scholarship. Finally, in her article, "Dismantling the Supercrip Prof: Theological Education and Faculty Accessibility," Natalie Wigg-Stevenson discusses the apparent contradictions between her and her students' access needs, illuminating the perils of disclosure for faculty in accommodations processes and calling for a broader culture of access in theological education that confronts conditions that undermine collective flourishing.

Indeed, several articles in the collection further expand our notions of both theological education and human flourishing by considering how neurodivergent people complicate philosophical theories and insights with respect to cultivating virtue and moral formation, especially when it comes to young people in congregations, society, and educational environments. In her article, "'Misfitting' and Friendship in the Virtuous Life: Neurodiversity and Moral Formation," Elizabeth Cochran argues that looking at autistic people through a deficit model has neglected the insights autistic people have for moral formation and Christian virtues. Drawing on Rosemarie Garland-Thomson's concept of "misfitting," as disabled persons' resisting and disrupting the norms of "fitting" in society (2011), Cochran argues that misfitting can be formational when it comes to virtues, especially those of compassion and justice. Reflecting on his own work with disabled youth in ministry, Benjamin T. Conner notes that there are "experiential, perspectival, and hermeneutical advantages" (p. 515) to disabled scholars' work in such fields. Although Conner discerns (for this reason among others) that he is not the person to write the next book on disability and youth ministry, he highlights how voice, vocation, and mental health are three important intersections for this ongoing work to explore. Finally, Michael Paul Cartledge and Erin Raffety draw on testimonies of neurodivergent youth, scholars, and practitioners to expand visions of what worship and prayer look like in God's brainforest, a euphemism for the brain that they borrow from educator Thomas Armstrong (2012). The metaphor of the brainforest disrupts the notion that our brains are to conform to a mechanistic standard and celebrates both a diversity of perspective individuals and an ecology of diversity in our congregations and classrooms that affirms the goodness of God's creation.

Because the emphasis in this collection is on construction, the articles do not engage the limits of the neurodiversity paradigm, often alleged to be an overly neurological focus or a tokenizing emphasis on diversity that acquiesces to neoliberalism. Yet, the truly diverse interpretations of this concept and its import for theological education perhaps already offer significant engagement with these critiques. And they also are just the beginning of the conversation. More intersectional perspectives when it comes to race and mental health are needed to further our understanding of neurodiversity and theological education. The conversation around neurodiversity in theological education tends to center autism in a way that neglects other experiences. More practical insights are needed from curriculum, students, and instructors to further our understanding of what is working and what is not. And more neurodivergent theologians are needed to conjure a fuller understanding of God, church, and academy. As this collection clarifies, however, diversity is not merely a feel-good concept. Neurodivergent perspectives further justice in calling account-ability to where access is limited for certain bodies and minds in church and academy spaces. In so doing, they do not just make spaces more accessible, but they deconstruct theologies that may not do justice to who God truly is. And as we reconstruct, may we do so as a diverse body of Christ that does not seek to conform to worldly ways but to be trans-formed by the renewing of our minds (Romans 12:2) in God's beloved brainforest.

Disclosure Statement

The authors declare there is no Complete of Interest at this study.

References

Armstrong, T. (2012). *Neurodiversity in the classroom: Strength-based strategies to help students with special needs succeed in school and life.* ASCD.

Fricker, M. (2007). *Epistemic injustice: Power and the ethics of knowing.* Oxford University Press.

Garland-Thomson, R. (2011). Misfits: A feminist materialist disability concept. *Hypatia,* *26*(3), 591–609. https://doi.org/10.1111/j.1527-2001.2011.01206.x

Walker, N. (2021). *Neuroqueer heresies: Notes on the neurodiversity paradigm, autistic empowerment, and postnormal possibilities.* Autonomous Press.

Theological Education with Neurodiversity in Mind: Research Insights and Future Possibilities

Michael Paul Cartledge and Erin Raffety

ABSTRACT
How might the neurodiversity paradigm and the stories of neurodivergent persons contribute to the work of theological education? Drawing on the insights of neurodivergent thinkers, worshipers, and ministry leaders, the authors outline a preliminary vision of theological education and Christian ministry that keeps neurodiversity in mind. The article begins by exploring the neurodiversity paradigm and discussing experiences of neurodivergence in congregational ministry. The authors then consider the task of theological education and the formation of leaders in light of the neurodiversity paradigm. Finally, the authors bear witness to new models of ministry that center the leadership of neurodivergent persons.

Introduction

We gathered at the Farminary, a former Christmas tree farm on Princeton Theological Seminary's campus where graduate students are invited to explore the connections among land, justice, soil, and neighbor.[1] We brought together a small group of young people, ages 12–16, with ADHD, Tourette's Syndrome, and other emotional and behavioral challenges, accompanied by their parents and youth ministers, to reflect together around the theme of variation in God's creation. Our goal for this event was a modest one: to learn about the experiences of neurodivergent youth in church and those who accompany them in their faith journey. As we worked together turning compost, collecting chicken eggs, and scattering seed, we discussed how the rich diversity in God's good creation reflects the beautiful variation in how we think, learn, and connect with God and neighbor.

This was the beginning of what became the Cultivating God's Brainforest project, an endeavor to develop an online course for youth workers to reimagine discipleship and faith formation with neurodiversity in mind.[2]

Drawing on our interviews with young people, as well as their families and ministers, we designed a five-module course that explores ministry through the lens of the neurodiversity paradigm, particularly as it is revealed in creation and community. But we also heard stories of hurt and pain when it came to lack of inclusion or rejection from church services or practices. Across the board, parents, neurodivergent youth, and youth ministers were struggling, because neurodivergent youth were too often perceived as a problem for the church to manage rather than people with challenges and gifts just like anyone else.

In our listening, research, and curriculum construction, it became clear that the neurodiversity paradigm had something important to offer in the training of ministers and the equipping of future theological educators. This article considers the aims and tasks of theological education in light of the neurodiversity paradigm, the history of the neurodiversity movement, and the work of neurodivergent ministers and educators. When we speak of theological education, we do so in an expansive sense, including ministry and education about God and Christian practices in both the church and the academy. Drawing on the insights of neurodivergent thinkers, worshipers, and ministry leaders, we seek to outline a preliminary vision of theological education and Christian ministry that keeps neurodiversity in mind. First, we will begin by exploring the neurodiversity paradigm, including language around the concept of neurodiversity and the history of the neurodiversity movement. Second, we will discuss experiences of neurodivergence in congregational ministry, centering the stories of young people. Third, we will consider the task of theological education and the formation of leaders and educators in light of the neurodiversity paradigm. Finally, we will highlight some emerging models of ministry that center the voices and leadership of neurodivergent persons to imagine a way forward.

Exploring neurodiversity

Many theological educators and ministry leaders might be unfamiliar with the term neurodiversity. When we began our work on the Cultivating God's Brainforest project, some conversation partners objected to the use of the term. Instead, we were advised to use language more familiar to the general public. To many, the term neurodiversity sounded too academic—something cooked up in the ivory tower. However, neurodiversity is not a scholarly concept, but a term that organically grew out of communities of neurodivergent thinkers and activists. It will be helpful here to offer a brief overview of the neurodiversity movement, along with some definitions of other commonly used terms like neurodivergence, neuronormativity, and neurominorities.

Nick Walker, a neurodivergent author, educator, and psychologist, defines neurodiversity as the "biological fact" of "the infinite variation in neurocognitive functioning within our species" (2021, p. 34). Simply put, neurodiversity is the reality that we all think, learn, experience the world, and connect with others in various ways. From a theological perspective, our Cultivating God's Brainforest project grounded the biological fact of neurodiversity in the goodness of variation in God's creation. The richness of diversity in creation is evident all around us, including within our faith communities (1 Cor. 12:12–31).

At its core, the Cultivating God's Brainforest course was designed to bring the work of youth ministry into conversation with the neurodiversity paradigm, which is a perspective on or approach to neurodiversity. While neurodivergent people think about the paradigm in diverse ways, Walker (2021) gives three fundamental principles of the neurodiversity paradigm. First, neurodiversity is a natural part of human variation. Second, there is no single, "right" way of thinking, learning, or behaving. And third, neurodiversity involves dynamics of social power similar to other forms of human diversity, such as ethnicity and gender. The neurodiversity paradigm stands in contrast to what has been called the pathology paradigm, which assumes there is a general "right" way of thinking, learning, and behaving. From the perspective of the pathology paradigm, "individuals and groups who fall outside dominant conceptions of normality, to what is deemed a clinically significant level at any given time or place, must be internally pathological" (Chapman, 2019, p. 373).

The three fundamental principles outlined above provide a foundation for what has been called the Neurodiversity Movement, which grew out of the Autism Rights Movement in the 1990s. Autistic activist and social scientist Judy Singer (1999) is often credited with coining the term neurodiversity, and Harvey Blume is thought to be the first to put the term into popular print in his article, "Don't Mourn for Us," which appeared in *The Atlantic* in 1998. The term quickly became a "rallying cry" for a new civil rights movement (Silberman, 2013), and it has become increasingly used in popular publications and across social media, where many neurodivergent persons find community and support.

The neurodiversity movement champions the rights of all neurodivergent persons; any person "having a mind that functions in ways which diverge significantly from the dominant societal standards of 'normal'" (Walker, 2021, p. 38). Neurodivergence is a broad term that includes various experiences and ways of being in the world, such as autism and ADHD, as well as other diagnoses and conditions like dyslexia and schizophrenia.[3] The *neuro* in neurodivergence might lead us to think only in terms individual brain function, but the Neurodiversity Movement has been squarely focused on the social realities of neurominorities: neurodivergent persons who share similar forms of neurodivergence that are part of their identities and often lead to some form of misunderstanding, prejudice, or discrimination from the neurotypical majority. Such discrimination stems from standards of neuronormativity, best understood as a culturally-constructed collection of norms around cognitive functioning and behavioral traits (see Walker, 2021). How might our own neurnormative assumptions and practices limit our imaginations around theological education and congregational ministry? This was one of the driving questions behind the Cultivating God's Brainforest project.

In light of the above question, we asked, what can the church learn from the neurodiversity movement, neurodivergent activists, and neurominorities within our communities? We linked the creation narrative, as an overarching theological framework, with Thomas Armstrong's (2012) conception of the "brainforest." Armstrong, a popular educator and author, employs this metaphor to emphasize the way human brains are more akin to rainforests than computers or machines. The theological framework of "God's brainforest" proved useful in responding to the neuronormativity that may be present within our congregations. While not wanting to push the metaphor too far, we believe the concept of the "brainforest" can be understood from both an individual and communal perspective, in which individual persons, as well as larger communities, reflect the beautiful variation found within a diverse ecosystem. For this reason, we use both neurodiverse youth and neurodivergent youth to emphasize both diverse and marginalized experiences of youth in church spaces.

Indeed, the first lesson of the curriculum, "Exploring God's Brainforest," begins with the caveat, "We might be committed to the belief that God calls God's creation 'good', but we often see aspects of variation and diversity as an inconvenience or even a burden," thus acknowledging the weight of neuronormativity for neurodivergent youth in church spaces (Cartledge & Raffety, 2022). The first lesson explicitly connects the beautiful, good diversity of God's creation (Gen. 1) with the body of Christ (1 Cor. 12:12–27). Although none of this work is theologically radical, it implicitly confronts the pathology paradigm that is so often the starting point for ministering or teaching about autism, ADHD, or other emotional and behavioral conditions. Furthermore, if neurodiverse youth are made good, just as they are, then their insights and experiences reflect who God is, their experiences help us see and know Jesus, and their disruptions point to the Holy Spirit, in ways we have only just yet to apprehend.

Congregational ministry and experiences of neurodivergence

What is it like, particularly for neurodivergent young people, to participate in congregational environments that are designed for neurotypical worshipers and learners? In our brief conversations with youth with mood disorders, Tourette's Syndrome, and other experiences of neurodivergence, youth bristled at the conformity often demanded in worship spaces. While one young person named Mo commented, "What I don't like about worship is the sermon. It can feel long and doesn't grasp my attention," she also went on to offer, "Whenever we're listening to the readings being read, I try to connect the stuff in the reading to things in my life that seem similar… It helps me understand better, and it helps me realize and care about it more deeply" (Mo, personal communication, February 3, 2022). When we hear neurodivergent youth critique the length of the sermon, it is easy to presume that their immaturity is to blame or that their attention span is limited. But what if these critiques invite us to examine practices in worship that may not be suitable for a variety of worshipers and learners, and that when expanded would add further access for more people, in general?

Erin Raffety (2022) argues that disabled worshipers can call the church to more active and participatory practices in worship, identifying where clerical paradigms (pastors preaching at congregants) both unintentionally passify congregations and restrict the active knowledge-making practices that the young person above suggests ("I try to connect the stuff in the readings to things in my life…") (pp. 133–34). Whereas needing to control or corral the energy and activities of youth in the service of worship positions youth or neurodivergent youth as the problem (see Conner, 2018), a neurodiversity paradigm affirms and appreciates different ways of being and engaging in worship, while also pointing toward multimodal ways of facilitating access. In Lesson 2 on "Prayer and Attention" in our curriculum, for instance, we begin with the insight that paying attention looks different for neurodivergent youth, which invites us to reconsider how our practices of prayer in worship often call for certain forms of attention, even while theologically, we believe prayer works because of the Spirit's intention (Hardwick, 2022b). Not only does this free us to more diverse, expansive practices of prayer (for instance, bodily movement, artwork, silence, or walking), but it draws us toward a more robust theology that does not rely on our right actions but places even the responsibility for prayer squarely on a good God who has created us just as we are.

Another young person with Tourette's commented,

> I like listening to all the church songs and being able to sing along with it. And like that can be pretty engaging. But I don't like standing in church. It's an odd thing, but it makes me have to focus on standing way more than focus on what we're actually doing or talking about. So, when I'm standing, I feel like, I feel like I'm focusing so hard on trying not to like sit down like as a tic, or tic more outwardly, I guess—something that would be more noticeable, because it seems to be more noticeable when I'm standing. So, it's hard to stand during worship. (Milo, personal communication, March 10, 2022)

When we played this audio clip for youth workers during the Princeton Forum on Youth Ministry in 2022, the response to these words was audible and affirming. "Wow, I had no idea," commented youth workers. "This really helps me better understand how something taken for granted like standing may be a burden in worship to a young person who is neurodivergent." Milo's testimony above speaks to the ways worship meaningfully engages the senses, but also to how embodied experiences may be internal, hidden, yet burdensome for neurodivergent youth. Indeed, the perception that neurodivergent youth are disengaged may cause neurotypical leadership to presume they do not want to be there at all.

One finding from our curriculum development experience was the importance of simply taking the time to ask. Our curriculum is peppered with testimonies like Mo's and Milos's, where they were quick to point out both what did and did not work in worship for them and other neurodiverse youth that they know. But all too often these perspectives are assumed, presumed, or taken for granted by adults and neurotypical folks in the church. The neurodiversity paradigm invites us to an attitude of unknowing when it comes to bodies, senses, and worship, making clear that if youth do not feel supported in our worship spaces, it is the church, not they, who is responsible for understanding what would make a meaningful difference. Therefore, the third lesson on "Worship and the Senses" in our curriculum highlights the Lutheran Synod of New Jersey's Joyful Noise worship ministry, a worship service geared toward neurodivergent children and their families. Although Joyful Noise was first developed for children and families, it is self-described as a service with all the typical elements of worship, geared toward all, but with "no boundaries," so that neurodivergent folks and families can be free to express themselves in worship (see Humm, 2022). The approach features a parachute accompanied by welcome music, opportunities for interaction and leadership for children and youth in scripture and communion service, a prayer rope that everyone grabs onto for the Lord's Prayer, fidget toys, and a quiet room for anyone who needs it.

We recall distinctly how Mo, whose family helped to start Joyful Noise, talked about how remarkable the service was, because it meant her whole family could be together in worship. Too often, families with neurodivergent youth are forced to "divide and conquer" by finding separate spaces that work for their families, because the typical worship service does not work well for several members. Mo's point helps put in perspective why a service like Joyful Noise may not be segregated as some perceive it, but working toward the full unity of the church in time. Raffety (2022) points out the value of such "free spaces" or disabled-led spaces, where folks who cannot participate or lead for one reason or another in typical spaces, find flourishing when boundaries are altered and their leadership is appreciated (pp. 136–137). These are different from segregated spaces, because they are sought out, created, and maintained by disabled people and their families. Indeed, by hosting such spaces the church honors these ministries by amplifying but not controlling the ministry and leadership of disabled people. It is important to point out that everyone in the congregation is invited to Joyful Noise, as well. It takes place at a time that does not compete with traditional worship services. Pastor Peter of Prince of Peace Lutheran Church, who presides over both the typical service and Joyful Noise services once a month on Sundays, talked about how humbled he was by the worship experience. He shared about the difference between proclaiming welcome to all and truly living that out, and this is one way to do so (Humm, 2022).

Just as neurodivergent youths' disconnect and discomfort in worship is too often perceived as their problem, the critical edge of ministries like Joyful Noise invite congregations to consider how (neuro)ableism may distort not just their Christian practices, but their very images of God and God's love. In her book, Raffety describes how even as the church covenanted to love her daughter, she in her heart of hearts wondered how someone who is disabled, nonspeaking, and nonambulatory might be capable of expressing and showing that love to others (pp. 8–10). Pondering this concern, Raffety highlights a subtle ableism in the misperception that simply because someone loves differently than us, that love is minimized or impoverished. Indeed, her experience as a parent involved being disabused of her own ableism, so that she could see and behold her daughter's love just as she gave and gives it.

In a scholarly conversation on "Neurodiversity and Youth Ministry" that we hosted in preparation for our curriculum development, Naomi Lawson Jacobs, independent religious scholar and neurodivergent disability advocate, shared that they often show love by speaking truth to power, as pushing for advocacy and reform. However, Jacobs went on to say that love can often be misperceived by the world as mere angst, criticism, or complaining. Vikram K. Jaswal and Nameera Akhtar (2018) have observed the ways in which neurotypical people shut down communication with neurodivergent people. For instance, when neurotypical people assume neurodivergent people are not interested in communicating because of things like echolalia or avoiding eye contact, they will actually turn away from neurodivergent people. Yet, these behaviors from neurodivergent folks may actually be bids for communication, in that neurodivergent people are using them to cope and maintain social interaction. In her research with churches, sociologist Krysia Waldock (2021) draws on the "double empathy problem" to explain how theories of the autistic mind as deficient and lacking in empathy necessarily impede non-autistic efforts at understanding and communicating with autistic people (see Milton et al., 2023).

This is where theories of neurodiversity are deeply needed to reframe differences in neurotypes as natural and widespread, thus also reframing communication as a complex, co-constructed effort (Raffety et al., 2019) rather than an act that reifies conventional values of empathy, love, and connection.

Raffety (2022) identifies how disabled people's cries against injustice can be silenced and shut out by churches in the name of decorum and propriety (pp. 87–98). But as she shows, through examples of the very public acts of lament by prophets in the Old Testament and disabled leaders, such as Bartimaeus in the New Testament, these are prophetic insights that the church badly needs to hear and is meant to hear. The fact that disabled people or neurodivergent people would show up and critique the church, rather than turn away given the myriad disconnects, hurts, and injustices, is an act of love and care, that shows a desire to make the church better. If our churches want to be a refuge to neurodivergent people, they must have the courage to bear witness to their pain and their critique, repent of their ableist biases in the aforementioned areas of prayer, worship, and connection, and nurture the ways neurodivergent people are calling forth new forms of ministry and leadership in our churches. Such a change begins with theological education.

Neurodiversity in the theological classroom

How might we reimagine the task of theological education in light of the neurodiversity paradigm and the stories and experiences of neurodivergent persons? As previously mentioned, we are using the term theological education in an expansive sense to mean ministry and education about God and Christian practices in both the church and the academy. But here let us briefly consider how the above stories of pain and lament have shaped our own pedagogy in the theological classroom. In his course on Neurodiversity, Faith Formation, and Young People at Princeton Theological Seminary, Michael Paul Cartledge has sought to give students space to reflect on their education and vocation in light of the neurodiversity paradigm and the witness of neurodivergent people. Students in this course have shared that too often theological education reinforces neuronormativity and excludes neurodivergent voices, and what is modeled in the theological classroom is often carried over into the context of congregational ministry. As one student commented, they are looking for "examples that could be integrated into their future congregational ministry," but "the status quo is very centered around texts and lectures, and students are expected to accommodate themselves to this model."

However, neurodivergent seminary students and ministry leaders are beginning to question the status quo in theological education. For instance, two neurodivergent students from Cartledge's neurodiversity and faith formation course have recently undertaken a project to reimagine teaching and studying biblical languages in light of the various ways students think and learn. Their efforts reflect a broader acknowledgement by many students that the neurodiversity paradigm does, indeed, have something to offer theological education, both for neurodiverse theology students and their neurodiverse congregations. In another recent example, a colleague who teaches homiletics shared that her students were questioning "standards" in preaching that seemed to reinforce neuronormative assumptions, such as the importance of direct eye contact. This reveals that a new cohort of ministry leaders are paying important attention to their own experiences and listening to stories of frustration and pain in their own congregational contexts.

How might theological educators foster environments for students to explore new models of ministry and challenge their own neuronormative assumptions? In the seminary classroom, one way this can be done is to incorporate diverse Christian practices into courses to help students experience a variety of ways to connect to God and neighbor. Following the lesson themes of attention, senses, and expression from the Cultivating God's Brainforest curriculum, we have sought to introduce practices and assignments that help students challenge the neuronormative status quo that may be present in their contexts. As stated above, it may be assumed that if someone has difficulty sitting still during a worship service, they are not paying attention. We might think that because someone prefers not to shake hands during the passing of the peace or keeps to themselves during social time before or after the church service, they are unfriendly. Such assumptions completely ignore the experiences and preferences of neurodivergent people in congregations, making participation in church a significant challenge. Introducing students to new practices of prayer, worship, and expression that challenge such assumptions can help students imagine new ways to push back on neuronormativity. Cartledge incorporates key elements of the Joyful Noise service, described above, such as the use of a prayer rope and parachute at the opening of class, to challenge students' expectations of class time and model practices that could be used in their own contexts. Additionally, drawing from practices from neurodivergent educators and fellow students, we model ways to check in with students at the start of class, such as color coded buttons, mood boards, and live polling.

It is crucial to provide theological students with opportunities to practice listening to stories such as those highlighted in the previous section. As one example of this, students in Cartledge's Neurodiversity, Faith Formation, and Young People course are given a "priestly listening" assignment, in which they are invited to conduct an informal interview around the topic of neurodiversity and ministry with a neurodivergent person, family member, or ministry leader. Osmer (2008) uses the term "priestly listening" to explain the descriptive-empirical task of practical theology, which "is grounded in a spirituality of presence" and "is a matter of attending to what is going on in the lives of individuals, families, and communities" (p. 34). The goal of this class assignment is to practice the invaluable skill of listening well and building connection, particularly where fracture may have occurred. What makes this a "priestly" activity is how it reflects "the twofold ministry of intercessory prayer," which involves "entering into the situation of others through personal contact, listening, and empathetic imagination," and then "placing their needs and concerns before God in prayer on their behalf" (p. 35). But this important skill is not for ministry leaders alone. Osmer states, "Priestly listening is, first and foremost, an activity of the entire Christian congregation as a fellowship in which people listen to one another as a form of mutual support, care, and edification" (p. 35). Thus, it is vital that Christian leaders be ready to model this skill in their ministry contexts, particularly with the support, care, and edification of neurodiverse communities in mind.

As we suggested in the previous section, providing space for purposeful sharing and lament invites those who have been wronged to cry out against those who have hurt them and it gives those in power an opportunity to have their hearts turned to prayer, as well (Raffety, 2022, pp. 83–86). The listening of the church to neurodivergent people requires action, such as witnessing, repenting, and nurturing. Theological educators can model this by making space in the classroom for students to share and reflect upon their own experiences. It is unsurprising that most students who take a course on neurodiversity and faith formation are deeply invested in the content because they or someone close to them identifies as neurodivergent and more often than not has experienced some kind of hurt in congregational ministry. When ministry leaders are shaped to listen well and foster environments that welcome diverse ways of prayer, worship, and expression, a new vision of congregational leadership may begin to emerge.

A vision of neurodivergent congregational leadership

One of the gifts of the neurodiversity paradigm for both ministry and theological education is that it lifts up broader varieties of human flourishing for the Kingdom of God. But so many of those testimonies to what flourishing looks like are just being uttered, stories are still to be written, let alone heard and received in our congregations. This is why, in the final lesson of our "Cultivating God's Brainforest" course, we amplified four testimonies from neurodiverse pastors and scholars, who shared what flourishing looks like for them. We heard from these leaders that flourishing is highly dependent on an environment that confronts neu-ronormativity and allies who come alongside neurodivergent people to amplify their gifts, as well as support them in the challenges they may face (Hardwick, 2022a). Furthermore, we heard that online environments may be particularly supportive for young people for whom in person worship and fellowship pose numerous barriers as illustrated above (Beck, 2022). When so many were languishing during the pandemic, some neu-rodivergent youth were thriving. We heard that inclusion is a dynamic rather than static process (Waldock, 2022), where congregations themselves need to be learning and adapting their approaches alongside neurodivergent leaders. Finally, we heard that too often neurodivergent leaders' gifts are pushed to the fringe of congregational life, and we all wondered, what would it look like to center them in our churches and schools?

One of the challenges in this work is that we lack the "mirrors" in the church (Raffety 2022), neurodivergent leaders, for youth and other neurodi-vergent folks to follow. For so many neurodivergent people, the journey through diagnosis and self-understanding is solitary and overwhelming (White, 2022), yet these very testimonies and the emergence of neurodiverse leadership within church spaces can be a catalyst for change. Raffety's paradigms of leadership, that of mirrors and accomplices (2022), provides somewhat of a template for how both neurodivergent and neurotypical people can participate in neurodi-verse flourishing for the Kingdom. Whereas given widespread neuronormativity, churches cannot act as mirrors for neurodivergent people, they can nurture neurodivergent leaders such that they can be mirrors and mentors for those who come after them. Meanwhile, drawing on autistic activist, Reyma McCoy McDeid, Raffety (2022) distinguishes between allies and accomplices, clarifying that allies often try to save individuals in a world that does not support them, whereas accomplices put some skin in the game, working alongside those they care about to change the system (pp. 191–192). In McDeid's words, "To be an ally is to help people who are marginalized in some capacity to make the most in this unchanged system," whereas, "To be an accomplice, on the other hand, is to work side by side with people who are marginalized, to confront the system and contribute to shifting it accordingly" (McDeid as cited in Ladau, 2021, p. 142).

This leadership paradigm both keeps neurodivergent people at the center of any ministry that seeks to serve them, and calls the church apart from mere inclusion (including neurodivergent people in church ministry that was not made for them) toward justice (working for change alongside dis-abled people and Jesus to change not just the church but the world) (Raffety, 2022). This means that centering neurodivergent voices moves away from a tokenizing or othering work of the church, by making churches accom-plices to Jesus' work of justice. When we re-envision disability ministry through the lens of Jesus' justice versus healing or inclusion, we behold the dignity Jesus desires to grant to disabled ministers and leaders, the myriad visions of the life abundant and human flourishing Jesus seeks to usher in, and the tearing down of neuronormative paradigms that Jesus centers as vital to any justice-making work for neurodivergent people.

Although such a vision remains abstract in it being but a vision for justice rather than a reality, Raffety (2022) also draws on fieldwork with disabled leaders to showcase some of their distinct misfitting, collaborative, and resourceful features (pp. 183–195). Rosemarie Garland-Thomson's concept of disabled "misfitting," the relational misfit between disabled people and the environments they live and work in, also exposes what she calls, "the fragility of fitting." In short, "Any of us can fit here today and misfit here tomorrow," she writes (2011, p. 597). The challenge for the church, then, becomes to receive the prophetic "misfit" of neurodiverse leadership rather than seek to correct, conform or fix it. Not only does misfitting prophetically signal and illuminate neuronormative structures and practices, but it also provides the potential for the formation of sub-jugated knowledges that lend value in the form of innovation, resource-fulness, and adaptability (Garland-Thomson, 2011, p. 604).

In her chapter on leadership, Raffety points to how the Clarke family, the originators of Joyful Noise, assert a misfitting, inverting process of normal-ization (Hart, 2014) as an aspect of their leadership. By leading *together* as a family in Joyful Noise spaces (As Mo says, "where my family can be together"), Special Olympics, and through their work with the Lutheran Synod of New Jersey, just to name a few, they insist that everyone should have access to a meaningful life with independence, choices, and social experiences. Although this does not seem radical, they draw on a strategy that Brendan Hart (2014), in his work with families with autistic children calls, "inverted normalization" (p. 293). By going together into neuronormative spaces and insisting that their children are not just tolerated but celebrated, the Clarkes challenge, test, and stretch the boundaries of what is normal.

But the creative, adaptive edge of misfitting is also evident in their leadership: they don't just challenge boundaries, they create new Christian worship practices by insisting that their leadership in Joyful Noise simul-taneously exist and resist within the space of the church. Thus, the mis-fitting qualities of Joyful Noise are active in that it both participates in Christian worship and refuses to conform to the practices of the typical service. Raffety describes the well-meaning efforts by the pastor at the Clarke's previous church to resolve this misfitting, or even capitalize on it, by creating children's worship programs. But the same pastor also acknowledges the mysterious wind-blowing of the Spirit, when she notes, "I see the Spirit moving, but I can't define it. With our Joyful Noise min-istry, I don't see us growing us this ministry like you would want to grow your church, I see this as a deepening" (p. 135).

Conclusion

Misfitting leadership can lead to deeper life in the Spirit, but American churches that are oriented toward growth and capitalism often fail to receive its gifts. Indeed, oriented toward individual, clergy-driven leadership, churches are often suspicious of the collaborative leadership of families like the Clarkes. "Why do you need Joyful Noise when you could all be together?" people will chide (Raffety, 2022, p. 143). And yet, the same churches will simultaneously bemoan the lack of lay leadership, the crumbling of liturgy and service amongst the people of the church (liturgy literally meaning in Greek "the work of the people") (Raffety, 2022, p. 69). This is where the critical, creative edge of misfitting leadership comes with a bang and not a whimper. Cries for justice within the very church that purports to effect it will make the church necessarily uncomfortable. Yet, resourcefulness may look more like being accomplices to a worthy crime than compliant acquiescors to the status quo. Going together, collaboratively, may be cumbersome in communities that prefer quick, able-bodied saviors. Calling the church, and theological education more broadly, toward a flourishing future will most certainly come with groaning. But let that not be groaning from the church. May the church and theological educators have the courage to truly go deeper with the Spirit, appreciating the gifts of neurodivergent, misfitting leadership in all their criticism, collaboration, and creativity.

Notes

1. This research received approval from the North Star Review Board in December 2021.
2. This project was part of Fuller Youth Institute's "Character-Forming Youth Discipleship" project, funded by The John Templeton Foundation. Learn more about the Cultivating God's Brainforest course at https://online.ptsem.edu/products/cultivating_Gods_brainforest.
3. It is important to note that not all people who experience mental distress identify as neurodivergent, such as those with bipolar disorder or schizophrenia, although the term is increasingly being used to include a wide variety of experiences and diagnoses.

Disclosure statement

No potential conflict of interest was reported by the authors.

References

Armstrong, T. (2012). *Neurodiversity in the classroom: Strength-based strategies to help students with special needs succeed in school and life.* ASCD.
Beck, S. (2022). Building trust online [video]. In *Cultivating God's Brainforest.* Princeton Theological Seminary. https://online.ptsem.edu/products/cultivating_Gods_brainforest

Cartledge, M., & Raffety, E. (2022). *Cultivating God's Brainforest* [course]. Princeton Theological Seminary. https://online.ptsem.edu/products/cultivating_Gods_brainforest

Chapman, R. (2019). Neurodiversity theory and its discontents: Autism, schizophrenia, and the social model of disability. In Ş. Tekin & R. Bluhm (Eds.), *The bloomsbury companion to philosophy of psychiatry* (1st ed., pp. 371–390). Bloomsbury Academic; Bloomsbury Collections.

Conner, B. (2018). *Disabling mission, enabling witness: Exploring missiology through the lens of disability studies.* InterVarsity Press.

Garland-Thomson, R. (2011). Misfits: A feminist materialist disability concept. *Hypatia, 26*(3), 591–609. http://www.jstor.org/stable/23016570 https://doi.org/10.1111/j.1527-2001.2011.01206.x

Hardwick, L. (2022a). Cultivating an Environment for Flourishing [video]. In *Cultivating God's Brainforest.* Princeton Theological Seminary. https://online.ptsem.edu/products/cultivating_Gods_brainforest

Hardwick, L. (2022b). The Spirit's intention [sermon]. In *Cultivating God's Brainforest.* Princeton Theological Seminary. https://online.ptsem.edu/products/cultivating_Gods_brainforest

Hart, B. (2014). Autism parents & neurodiversity: Radical translation, joint embodiment and the prosthetic environment. *BioSocieties, 9*(3), 284–303. https://doi.org/10.1057/biosoc.2014.20

Humm, R. (2022). Joyful noise introduction [video]. *Vimeo.* https://vimeo.com/799232894/aed3aacc12

Jaswal, V., & Akhtar, N. (2018). Being versus appearing socially uninterested: Challenging assumptions about social motivation in autism. *The Behavioral and Brain Sciences, 42,* E82. https://doi.org/10.1017/S0140525X18001826

Ladau, E. (2021). *Demystifying disability: What to know, what to say, and how to be an ally.* Ten Speed Press.

Milton, D. E. M., Waldock, K., & Keates, N. (2023). Autism and the "double empathy" problem. In F. Mezzenzana & D. Peluso (Eds.), *Conversations on empathy: Interdisciplinary Perspectives on imagination and radical othering* (pp. 78–97). Taylor & Francis.

Osmer, R. (2008). *Practical theology: An introduction.* Eerdmans Publishing.

Raffety, E. (2022). *From inclusion to justice: Disability, congregational ministry, and leadership.* Baylor University Press.

Raffety, E., Vollrath, K., Harris, E., & Foote, L. (2019). Lonely joy: How families with nonverbal children with disabilities communicate, collaborate, and resist in a world that values words. *Journal of Pastoral Theology, 29*(2), 101–115. https://doi.org/10.1080/10649867.2019.1621024

Silberman, S. (2013, April 16). Neurodiversity rewires conventional thinking about brains. *WIRED.* https://www.wired.com/2013/04/neurodiversity/

Sinclair, J. (1993). Don't mourn for us. *Our Voice, 1*(3), n.p.

Singer, J. (1999). Why can't you be normal for once in your life?: From a 'Problem with No Name' to a new category of disability. In M. Corker & S. French (Eds.), *Disability Discourse* (pp. 59–67). UK: Open University Press.

Waldock, K. (2021). "Doing church" during COVID-19: An autistic reflection on online church. *Canadian Journal of Theology, Mental Health and Disability, 1*(1), 66–70.

Waldock, K. (2022). Flourishing on the fringes [video]. In *Cultivating God's Brainforest.* Princeton Theological Seminary. https://online.ptsem.edu/products/cultivating_Gods_brainforest

Walker, N. (2021). *Neuroqueer heresies: Notes on the neurodiversity paradigm, autistic empowerment, and postnormal possibilities.* Autonomous Press.

White, E. (2022). Learning to celebrate my brain [video]. In *Cultivating God's Brainforest.* Princeton Theological Seminary. https://online.ptsem.edu/products/cultivating_Gods_brainforest

Speaking with Us, Not for Us: Neurodiversity, Theology and Justice

Naomi Lawson Jacobs 🆔

ABSTRACT

To belong in the Christian tradition, we must be able to contribute to it. Yet neurodivergent Christians have rarely been enabled to tell our own stories about ourselves as a vital part of God's (neuro)diverse creation. In common with other autism research, academic theology is framed by pathologizing clinical paradigms of autism; neurodivergent people's situated knowledge about ourselves has not always been valued in the field. In this aut-ethnography, I use reflections from a decade of engaging with autism theology – often a painful experience of Othering – to frame a response informed by critical autism and neurodiversity studies. Drawing on lived theology from autistic research participants, I consider what our neurodiversity theologies have to offer to academic theology. Finally, I ask how theologians can do justly by speaking with, not for, neurodivergent people.

Friday, 3 PM.

I'm in the library, surrounded by books of theology about autism, and I'm shaking.

Many of these books share narratives of autistic people, whom the writers clearly love – telling their stories for them. Other authors are just speaking for us. (For me.)

Assuming the voice of God, some theologians say I am the result of a Fallen world. That people like me didn't exist in Eden. They tell me to celebrate, because I will be cured in Heaven!

(What do you want me to do for you? they forget to ask. If they were listening, the answer would not be, "Make me neurotypical.")

I'm told that to call myself disabled and autistic is to be misrecognized. That these are not my true names.

(I remember a powerful moment, when neurodivergent speaker Jemma said "Disability is part of our identity in Christ, and that's something to be celebrated.")[1]

Some books debate whether I am a person. For hundreds of pages.

(In my fragile bones, I feel the weight of history, of all the times people like me didn't count as human, from mass institutionalisation to eugenics.)

Over and over, medical and psychological research is used to explain away my reality.

(The writers don't talk about the harm clinical research has done to autistic people. They don't share our own, very different stories about ourselves.)

All the books, even the most well-meaning ones, discuss me as a problem to be solved. They toss me back and forth like a theological football, till I'm battered and bruised and exhausted. They write for neurotypical people, not for me.

But I have to keep pushing myself through this pile of unsafe books, for fear of being accused of not engaging with the literature.

Stories have power.

This is not my story.[2]

—

1: Speaker/s and know/ers

I am an "unreliable narrator" (Yergeau, 2013). Defined by others, disbelieved when I tell my story, excluded from the conversation about me. Being autistic "signifies fundamental nonexistence" in our ableist, neuronormative culture (Yergeau, 2013).[3] This is a belief with deep cultural roots, and it permeates the stories told about neurodivergent people.[4]

About people like me.

I do not recognize myself in the stories most theologians tell about me. I spent seven years in the wilderness, afraid to cross the threshold of a church, and my alienation began amidst these stories. Theologies where I became "them"—where I was both the subject and object of theology (Campbell, 2009, p. 122).[5] Autism has been a concern of pastoral theology for a decade and a half (Swinton & Trevett, 2009), but neurodivergent people ourselves have rarely been enabled to tell our own stories of church, faith and our place in God's (neuro)diverse creation.

"It is a fraught thing to hear yourself described and debated, especially by those who do not share your identity" (Boot, 2022).

This is epistemic injustice (Fricker, 2007).[6] And in this, the church is a mirror of society. Neurodivergent people have long been the objects of others' knowledge (Botha & Cage, 2022; Milton, 2017, p. 124; Walker, 2021, p. 94). Our *knowing* about ourselves has not been valued (Chapman & Botha, 2023; Stone & Priestley, 1996). My credibility as an autistic person is doubted; my "account of everyday experiences and harms" is disbelieved (Chapman & Carel, 2022, p. 2). If I speak, I cannot *really* be autistic (Chapman & Carel, 2022). If I do not speak, my silence is a tragedy—not a repression of my voice—and someone else will tell my story for me (Davis, 1995; Jacobs, 2018; Michalko, 2002).

My autistic narrative is fragmented. I do not write in straight lines. Silenced by a world and a church that cannot hear my voice, I can easily forget that God speaks through this autistic, ADHDer, dyspraxic body-mind (Belser, 2019; Raffety, 2020).

"Participation in the great story of salvation that is enacted and spoken about in church and faith community is prevented. Silence is all that remains" (Williams, 2022, p. 195).[7]

> Lucy: I've only told one person at church that I have Asperger's and she told me I was wrong. So I didn't tell anyone else.
>
> Naomi: Wrong in what sense?
>
> Lucy: She said, "No you don't. You can't have that." So I didn't tell anyone again.
>
> – Extract from an interview with Lucy (Jacobs, 2018)

In writing an aut-ethnography about my experiences of reading theology as a neurodivergent person, I am speaking back to those who would speak about me without me (Denzin, 2014). Autoethnography is a research method that uses personal experience to show how "the researcher and the social world impact on each other" (Pitard, 2017). In *aut-ethnography*, autistic people reclaim our fragmented, "rhizome-esque" stories (Milton, 2017, p. 105), resisting cultural narratives that can only imagine us as silent (Yergeau, 2013).

This is my story.

Two other neurodivergent people speak in this article: Lucy and Anthony, autistic participants in my research with disabled Christians (Jacobs, 2018).[8] Lucy is also dyspraxic. Like me, they speak differently,[9] and their stories have often been invalidated. These are neurodiversity theologians worth listening to.

> I've not been going to [the house group] for that long there, so I've—I've not really spoken much yet. I, kind of, offer to read the passage and then I figure I've got some speaking in…
>
> I've got a rubbish memory. I—it's terrible, so when I'm reading stuff, I don't remember, kind of, other stuff that I've read… I think it makes my faith really, kind of, surface. It doesn't go as deep as other people's seem to, if that makes sense, where they've got more understanding of things.
>
> – Lucy

I know how the trauma of misfitting[10] *in a neuronormative world can leave you feeling like your faith is not good enough, Lucy. All because you cannot communicate and think in the 'right' ways. Later, you will share your vision of a (neuro)diverse Heaven, and it won't matter if you don't remember all the right words. God speaks through your experience.*

I do not aim to speak *for* anyone except myself, but I hope to speak *with* my neurodivergent community (Crowder, 2022). As I shift between "we," "I" and "they" (Kafer, 2013), I aim to "point towards a new discursive space [for] autistic-led commentary that responds to and moves with... the diversifying autistic voices of our times" (Crowder, 2022, p. 71). I write as an autistic, dyspraxic ADHDer and disabled person, as a precariously self-employed researcher in disability and religious studies, and as an edge-walker on the margins of the institutional church (Waldock, 2021). I model language, rather than debating it,[11] citing neurodivergent writers on the terms that have emerged from our community, from *neurodiversity* (Singer, 2016) to *neurominority* (Walker, 2021, p. 21).[12] Language matters, but a shared language "means very little, if next you are denying autistic people complex emotions, identity, community, culture, and objectifying and othering them" (Botha & Cage, 2022).

Sometimes, when I have been silenced beyond what I can stand, God is in the silence.

2: Knowing neurodiversity

I speak, halting and clumsy, panic-scrambling to script a string of words, force them out in an order you will recognize. I lose words. I know the name of the theory but the wrong one is all that will come out of my mouth. This is an academic presentation, and I am being judged on whether I can speak convincingly enough to fit in a neurotypical academy.

"You talk about 'disability' and 'neurodiversity'—" I can hear the quotation marks "—but aren't we all the same in the sight of God? Aren't we all a little bit autistic?"

It is not God's eyes that freeze me now. I fight down my body's need to rock and shake. Bite the skin around my fingers so hard they bleed.

"You say you speak as an autistic person—"

Fragile neural circuits shatter under pressure.

"—but you can speak."

And I am silence/d.

—

I live in a society which imagines people like me as a public health crisis (Bumiller, 2008). Academic research into autism and other neuro-divergences is dominated by a dehumanizing pathology paradigm, which imagines neurodivergent people as 'disordered' and seeks to 'cure' our differences (Botha & Cage, 2022; O'Dell et al., 2016).[13] Research marginalizes our knowledge of ourselves, rather than imagining we might have insights into the lived experience of neurodivergence (Botha & Cage, 2022; Luterman, 2019; Milton, 2017; Walker, 2021). Most autism research still defines me by the absent self theory (Bustion, 2017; Frith, 2008), which says I have no ability to empathize with others, no 'theory of mind' (Baron-Cohen, 1997).

"How can one defend her own humanity if she does not recognize the humanity of others?" (Yergeau, 2013).

The pathology paradigm is rooted in a destructive fiction of what it means to be human (Deligny, 2015; Milton, 2017, p. 104)—a norm against which neurominorities fall short (Bowman, 2021; Walker, 2021). Divergent neurotypes, such as autism, are "widely taken to be at odds... with living a good human life" (Chapman & Carel, 2022, p. 3).

Naomi: Have you felt that you're accepted as you are [at your church]?

Lucy: It's been, kind of, mixed. I think in some ways I have been. And in others I get this, you know, this expectation that everyone should be really involved and should be going to, you know, so many things and should have a good circle of friends, and some things that I don't have and others I don't want.

And because our own voices are not heard in most research, research rarely asks how we can be given the opportunity to live up to our potential *as neurodivergent people* (Chapman & Carel, 2022, p. 2). Epistemic injustice stifles our flourishing, as the people God created us to be.

Engaging with research that has literally denied I am a person can be very painful (Luterman, 2019). But neurodivergent people are speaking back against epistemic injustice.

Critical autism studies and neurodiversity studies are challenging the power of research to construct us without us (Botha & Cage, 2022; Huijg, 2020; Mueller, 2020; O'Dell et al., 2016). Neurodivergent researchers are highlighting the abusive 'interventions' that result when research represents neurodivergence as abnormal and less than human (O'Dell et al., 2016; Walker, 2021). They are challenging misrepresentations of autistic people's existence (e.g. Murray et al., 2005), countering the harmful idea that we lack 'theory of mind' with the 'double empathy problem' (Milton, 2017).[14] In the face of invalidating questions asking us for whom we speak (Milton, 2019), the neurodiversity movement continues to make a stand against research and theory that has the power to cause suffering and inequality (Silberman, 2015; Yergeau, 2013). Our critiques are about justice.

Our own research is rooted in the neurodiversity paradigm (Walker, 2021)—a philosophy that celebrates our different ways of being and thinking. Neurodiversity is natural, valuable, and essential to human flourishing (Milton, 2020). At the same time, the neurodiversity paradigm acknowledges that we are marginalized neurominorities (Walker, 2021, p. 43), in a society designed to sustain neurotypical people's needs (Milton, 2020; Silberman, 2015). The concept of neurodiversity gives us tools to challenge our marginalization.

3: Neurodiversity and theology

I was so excited to find a theology article on whether Peter might have had ADHD. It's something that I and other neurodivergent people have pondered, imagining Peter as one of our people.[15] Peter is my relatably distractible, gloriously impulsive, saying-what-no-one-else-dares-to, deeply-feeling, holy-loving, prophetic ADHDer hero, and his neurodivergence just might be critical in the history of the church. So maybe my neurodivergence matters to God too.

But, among some nice conclusions about including easily-distracted people in church, I read that "Peter's story may in fact cause us to ask if the whole body of Christ has ADHD in a metaphorical sense."[16] (I am not your metaphor.) Peter's difference is erased. His neurodivergence doesn't matter. By the end of the article, ADHDer Peter has become just another a lesson in patience and grace for neurotypical people. And I've lost the neurodivergent saint I needed.

He, and I, are silenced.

—

Theology need not be rooted in pathology paradigms. We have been blessed with very different ways of thinking about diversity, from critical disability theologians (Betcher, 2007; Bowman, 2021; Eiesland, 1994; Hardwick, 2021)[17] who see disabled and neurodivergent people as part of "the beautiful biodiversity that God has woven throughout the tapestry of creation" (Kenny, 2022, p. 155). Inspired by them, I embrace the neurodiversity paradigm as a theological vision—of the glorious neurological diversity of God's human creation, and the uniqueness of the *imago Dei* in each of us.

"This is who I am and how God created me" (Hardwick, 2021, p. 11).

What a liberating image of the divine, when all I have ever heard are stories of a neurotypical God. A God who can create such diversity might be an autistic ADHDer like me. The idea makes me rock happily in my library seat, and for once, I don't care who sees. Maybe I won't be eradicated in Heaven. Maybe I'll meet a neurodivergent God there, and we'll recognize each other (Jacobs & Richardson, 2022).

Yet, as autistic pastor Lamar Hardwick warns us, "The Christian understanding of faith, sin, salvation, and all that we believe begins with a simple story about the dangers of desperately wanting to rid ourselves of our humanity" (2021, p. 9). So much pastoral theology is rooted in pathologizing clinical theories of autism (Bustion, 2017), dominated by outdated representations of me as an absent self (e.g. Brock, 2019; Cox, 2017; Dearey, 2009; Deeley, 2009; Dubin & Graetz, 2009; Evers, 2017; Hauerwas, 2013; Lewis, 2009; Swinton, 2012). Scientific abstractions distance philosophical concepts from people (O'Dell et al., 2016; Yergeau, 2013); I read far more debate about *autism* and what it means for neurotypical people than I hear *autistic people's* perspectives (e.g. Brock, 2019; Cox, 2017; Gillibrand, 2014; Harshaw, 2012; Leidenhag, 2022). The question of whether I am human is kept alive by well-meaning but abstracted debate about selfhood, personhood and the *imago Dei* (Cox, 2017; Gillibrand, 2014; Gordon, 2009; Hills et al., 2019; Leidenhag, 2021). Euphemisms deny I am part of God's (neuro)diverse creation (Walker, 2021); phrases such as "a person who lives with the experience of autism" (Tam, 2022, p. 25) represent my different ways of being as a terrible cross to bear.[18] I am told my neurodivergent experience and identity are little more than a label (Brock, 2019; Edmonds, 2011), by those who have not heard my story of how my life and faith were transformed when I first named myself an *autistic person*, created by God, just as I am.

"When I receive messages from church members implying that I should avoid labeling myself as autistic, it both breaks my heart and opens my eyes to the reality that the church has so much to learn" (Hardwick, 2021, p. 8).

This is a field dominated by "the perspectives of nonautistic parents and church communities to the exclusion of the perspectives of autistic persons themselves" (Bustion, 2017, pp. 661–662). Theology is overwhelmingly concerned with non-speaking autistic people, often conflated with those with learning disabilities (e.g. Brock, 2019; Gillibrand, 2014; Hills et al., 2019; Lewis, 2009; Tam, 2021, 2022).[19] But speaking and non-speaking are complex and shifting for us; speech has little to do with intelligence or support needs, and autistic people communicate in diverse ways (Botha et al., 2023).[20] Theologians expressing solidarity with autistic people who do not use speech can easily fall into the trap of filling the 'gaps' of their silence to legitimize theologies (Jacobs, 2018; Raffety, 2021). This may make it easier to dismiss those who communicate through speech or writing, and our critiques (e.g. Evers, 2017; Harshaw, 2012; Hills et al., 2019; Lewis, 2009). At the same time, I see the vitally important concept of lived experience appropriated or denied in theology, so that neurotypical professionals may continue to speak for us (e.g. Brock, 2019; Harshaw, 2012).

Amidst the theological interest in remembering that we are all one in Christ, my difference and identity are downplayed or erased (e.g. Barclay, 2008; Brock, 2019; Macaskill, 2019; Swinton, 2011). I become a metaphor for Christianity to think with (Betcher, 2007, p. 59; e.g. Brock, 2019; Dearey, 2009; Gillibrand, 2014; Gordon, 2009; Leidenhag, 2022). I still see more than a hint of the instrumental use (Hull, 2014) of autistic people in theology, as though we are here to bring the rest of the church closer to God (e.g. Barclay, 2008; Brock, 2009; Hills et al., 2019; Shrier, 2018; Swinton, 2012; Tam, 2022).[21] I read that I may need to repent of using my autistic identity as an excuse for my different ways of being (Macaskill, 2019, p. 436)—reminding me of years of judgment from fellow Christians, whose comfort has been disrupted by my difference (Spies, 2021)—but rarely do I read theology calling for neurotypical Christians to repent of the systemic exclusion of neurodivergent people from their churches.[22]

At the other end of this Othering, I come to "signify what it means to be inhuman" (Yergeau, 2013).

Like other autism research (Botha & Cage, 2022; Luterman, 2019), theology of autism is beginning to respond to autistic people's critiques. Academic theologians are beginning to ask autistic people about their own experiences of church, faith and spirituality (Burnett, 2021; Rapley, 2021; Tam, 2021; van Ommen & Endress, 2022).[23] A few theologians are challenging theology's own history of dehumanizing us (Leidenhag, 2021, 2022), questioning deficit-based paradigms of autism (Macaskill, 2019) and responding to autistic people who have been harmed or marginalized by churches, challenging the church to do better (Macaskill, 2019; van Ommen & Endress, 2022).

Yet theology still overwhelmingly speaks about us, without us.[24]

God is in the silence. Not in the silencing.

This is part of a broader trend in pastoral theology of disability, which has often talked about disabled people without centering our perspectives (Betcher, 2007; Jacobs, 2018; Lewis, 2007). Pastoral theology focuses on the care of autistic people (Brock, 2019; Burnett, 2021; Tam, 2021), but has less to say about barriers to belonging in churches (Waldock, 2023). When theology distances autism from disability (Leidenhag, 2021; van Ommen & Endress, 2022),[25] and rejects disability theory as irrelevant to churches (Brock, 2019; Edmonds, 2011; Evers, 2017; Swinton, 2011), it becomes harder for neurodivergent people to represent ourselves differently.[26] Secondhand stories about relationships with autistic people are common in theology (e.g. Brock, 2019; Gillibrand, 2014; Harshaw, 2012; Tam, 2021),[27] but neurotypical theologians have not often been reflexive about their power in this conversation (Campbell, 2009; Jacobs & Richardson, 2022), even as a few autistic theologians begin to identify themselves (Macaskill, 2019; Rapley, 2021; Williams, 2022). And on all divergent neurotypes other than autism—ADHD, dyspraxia, dyslexia, Tourette's Syndrome—academic theology is largely silent.[28]

Instead, theology imagines churches as ideal Christian communities where neurodivergent people will find welcome and friendship (Brock, 2019; Burnett, 2021; Swinton, 2012; Tam, 2022). Yet I read few stories of neurodivergent people like me, who have been traumatized and alienated by church communities. Nor do I often hear about those of us who are differently social,[29] and might prefer to seek God alone, in the quiet places to which Jesus also withdrew.

> Naomi: You just don't want to take part?

> Anthony: Exactly, yes. Which is why the most comfortable way I find to take my faith is all in there, you know, in my head, because at any time, you know, in prayer I can ask for God's help, I can ask for forgiveness, whatever it might be.

In a neurotypical vision of friendship in theology of autism, I read that I must assimilate into neuronormative social Christian communities. This is a model of inclusion, not justice (Jacobs & Richardson, 2022; Raffety, 2022), where neurotypical churches set the terms for my hospitality (Jacobs, 2018). And I wonder when I will hear not charitable calls to be 'friends' with me, but outrage at the injustices that keep me from belonging in churches at all.

My neurodivergent participants had a different way of *knowing* about social churches.

> Naomi: Can you imagine an environment where you would be more comfortable in a church—if not completely comfortable, then more than you have been?

> Anthony: ...When I say I don't have to go to a church to [have faith], that should not be interpreted as saying, "I don't think the church has any purpose at all," because I certainly think it does. But a lot of the church's work is invariably and quite understandably pretty social... Which in many ways is an absolutely wonderful thing, because it sort of, brings a lot of pleasure to a lot of people that way, gives them a sense of wellbeing and happiness, which has to be a good thing. Except of course everyone is different, and I'm in the minority on the other end of the scale who is much more of a loner, and quite enjoys solitude... But at the same time I can completely understand if other people had to live in that manner like I do, they'd go completely out of their minds, in the same way I would if I was having to do, you know, social things like that all the time, which I'd find extremely exhausting.

Imagine if neurotypical-led church communities could empathize with neurodivergent people as strongly as Anthony empathized with his neurotypical fellow Christians.[30] Anthony's vision of justice meant justice for all God's people—even if that meant there was no place for him in church communities. But he did not give up on the idea of a church that could honor and enable the flourishing of autistic Christians too.

> Just because we've always done something this way, doesn't mean that we always have to, if there's a better way, and I think there is.

> – Anthony

Anthony's failure to belong made space for new narratives (May, 2011) about more just ways of doing church. He and Lucy resisted silencing.

They spoke back, sharing their embodied, lived theology, as neurodivergent *knowers*.

"Perhaps this is something like what the apostle Paul means at the end of 1 Corinthians 12, when he writes, 'I will show you the most excellent way'" (2021, p. 130).

I long for churches where Lucy and Anthony's different, neurodivergent ways of being and *knowing* are valued, not as objects of charitable outreach, but as transformative witness to the (neuro)diversity of God's Kingdom.

4: Doing justly

"I think it's very worrying, the approach you're taking in this research," the senior professor says.

I think she's angry about my argument that disabled people should be able to speak for ourselves, but it's hard to be sure. There is a chasm between her and me, too deep to be ever bridged by words.

And God hovered over the waters of the deep.

"My sister is a cripple," the senior professor says. "Her affliction is very hard for me."

I drop my water bottle. It goes rolling, spinning away, under the wheels of my wheelchair. My support worker reaches down to pick it up. Later, she will write a witness statement, and she will be believed, because she's neurotypical and non-disabled.

But I cannot speak.

—

To belong in the Christian tradition, we must be able to contribute to it.[31]

It matters whose stories are told, and who tells them.[32] The idea of lived experience is contested in theology, even co-opted to speak for marginalized groups (Radford, 2022). But our embodied experience, as marginalized people, is a vital way of *knowing* about God, the Bible and church (Chopp, 1987; Cone, 1975).

"Autistic writers write autism differently because our brains work differently" (Bowman, 2021, p. 220).

Theology that does not center neurodivergent people's embodied experience will be unable to hear the very different questions we are asking—about access, participation and (in)justice in churches (Jacobs & Richardson, 2022, p. 124).[33]

> The small group now, we just, kind of, read [the Bible passage] and people answer the question. And if I don't understand it, then, well, I just never understand it... I think that people would, kind of, be open to [other ways of responding to the passage] being suggested, but... the majority of people would never suggest that, because they can understand it... The couple of people that might find it useful either have never thought of that or wouldn't dare suggest it.
>
> – Lucy

"If I don't understand it, then, well, I just never understand it." Lucy's words convict me, as someone with educational privilege, who understands a hostile world by studying it. I wonder how many other neurodivergent people don't "dare" ask for a different way of understanding the Christian tradition. Neurodivergent Christians cannot join the conversation about us until it is accessible to us.

> I think my concept of normal is, it doesn't actually exist anyway. And it's all the people who make the rules, who perhaps, I don't know, define normal as what they are, and form their rules based on the opinions accordingly. Without often consulting anyone else who is not, in inverted commas, 'normal.'
>
> – Anthony

Reflecting on the power of neurotypical people and perspectives in churches, Anthony added, "It's sort of a question again of them having to learn about us, and us having to learn about them." As he reminds us that we all need to work to overcome the double empathy problem, Anthony begins to guide us toward ways that theologians can *do justly* in research with neurodivergent people.

Theologians can do justly by recentering neurodivergent voices in the theological conversation. We can offer a Christian challenge to the academic ableism and barriers (Brown & Leigh, 2020; Martin, 2020) that keep neurodivergent people from contributing to theology.[34] We can undertake participatory research that builds interactional expertise with autistic and other neurodivergent people (Milton, 2017), "not merely as sources of empirical material, but as active participants in the production of knowledge on autism" (Milton & Bracher, 2013, p. 61). And we can teach a diverse curriculum that includes neurodiversity and critical disability perspectives, welcoming critique from the grassroots (Ahmed, 2000, 2017). As we share our power, theologians may be inspired to examine our imposed theology (Marti, 2016) and our paradigms of neurodiversity, and to be led by neurodivergent people's embodied understandings of God.

Theologians can also amplify an emerging neurodiversity theology, bursting into being outside the inaccessible towers of academia (Allison, 2019, 2021; Hartley, 2019; Memmott, 2019; Memmott & Noël, 2020; Noël & MacMillan, 2022).[35] They can support a small but growing number of neurodivergent scholars shaping neurodiversity theology (Bowman, 2021; Morgan, 2022; Waldock, 2021; Williams, 2022), and the critical autism scholars offering theologians new ways to think with, not about, autistic people (Bustion, 2017; Waldock & Forrester-Jones, 2020). These are our "threshold theologies" (Jacobs, 2018; Muers & Grant, 2017), our holy disruption on the margins of the church (Spies, 2021). Inspired by the neurodiversity paradigm, we are telling each other new stories about God's (neuro)diverse creation, about a God like us (Jacobs & Richardson, 2022).

These are stories I recognize myself in.

Only when neurodivergent people are imagined as theologians, as storytellers, as *knowers,* will we discover what our neurodiversity perspectives have to offer theology.

> I have thought about [healing and disability in heaven] actually. I didn't work out what the answer was. But I think I came to a middle where I thought that there'd either be healing or it wouldn't be a problem. So, you know, other people's attitudes or whatever it is that gets in the way... I don't think all disabilities are necessarily a problem. So if they're not a problem, why would they be fixed? Because a lot of things... it's just a word to describe something that's a bit more than your character, but it's related to that... It's more other people that—If other people's imperfections get in the way then it might be those that are changed.
>
> – Lucy

In spite of all the barriers they faced to belonging in churches, Lucy and Anthony were clear that *they* are not problems that need solving, fixing or curing. It is a neuronormative society and church that needs to change. Their neurodiversity theology and eschatology did not re-rehearse the question of whether neurodivergent people are human, whether we are created in the image of God. They centered neurodivergent flourishing. Speaking from embodied lived experience, Lucy and Anthony asserted that they are a vital part of God's (neuro)diverse creation.

When I listen to Anthony and Lucy, I remember that I am created by God as I am, and that my God-given identity as an autistic ADHDer *matters*. With my neurodivergent community, "I learn to love my neighbor because I keep learning to love myself" (Bowman, 2021, p. 242).

The wilderness makes space for new stories. Through our embodied neurodiversity theology, we are calling theologians to think differently about us... and about God.

To speak with us, not for us.

—

Library. Friday, 5 PM.

There's a book in my bag that I have higher hopes for. I bought it because one contributor is autistic. Claire Williams has written a powerful autoethnography here – a narrative about neuronormative churches and how they traumatize her.

She speaks of "a silence that transcends the ability to speak in any given moment; it is the silence of having no story to tell – no ability to place oneself within the charismatic narrative of glory."[36]

Her story resonates into my shaken, fragile bones, through a body and mind that carry trauma like hers. As she finds God in the silence, she speaks back against the silencing.

"God is not found in the noise and external action... God offers a hopeful encounter via presence. Elijah participates by being fully himself."[37]

She is speaking with me.

When I read neurodivergent and disabled theologians, I'm more likely to trust that I'm safe among their words. Naive? Maybe. Hearing "I am like you" doesn't guarantee that their writing won't traumatize me. But this is a numbers game. And so far, my embodied experience has been reflected most often in the lived theologies of other Deaf, disabled and neurodivergent people. That's no surprise, when they share so much of my story – the ableism we meet with in churches; the trauma waiting for us inside the gates; the exclusion, when churches close those heavy gates to us.

The silencing.

This personal and communal history of trauma – this longing for safety in numbers – is one reason why some of us ask if a Christian event on disability or neurodiversity is disabled-led. It's not an accusation. I think we just want to know if we'll be safe. Please, give us grace, and tell us you will listen to our story.

"I am not waiting for a brighter future where I am not myself, rather I am being. I am existing in the crip time of Holy Saturday."[38]

With Williams, I find God in the holy silence of Holy Saturday. But still I long for the not-yet of the Kingdom, where we confront the silencing that does not make room for God's voice. One day, I want to wake up in a world where there are more people like me at the table, speaking back. More Deaf, disabled and neurodivergent theologians (and poets and memoirists and social researchers and artists and TikTokkers). Non-disabled and neurotypical allies, too, listening and amplifying our voices. Until there are so many of us that everyone else has to sit up and take notice, when we ask, Where are our stories?

A more just world, yes.

But also a safer world.[39]

Notes

1. Jemma Brown (Richardson et al., 2022).
2. Adapted from my blog post *Safety In Numbers: Autism, Theology and Me* (Jacobs, 2022).
3. Neuronormativity is "the performance of the local dominant culture's current prevailing images of how a so-called 'normal' person with a so-called 'normal' mind thinks and looks and behaves" (Walker, 2021, p. 53).
4. The neurodiversity movement grew out of the autism self-advocacy movement, but the concept of neurodivergence is used today by people with ADHD, by dyslexic, dyspraxic and dyscalculic people, by those with Tourette's Syndrome, and increasingly by people with learning disabilities and/or mental and emotional distress (Graby, 2015). Responding to critiques that the neurodiversity paradigm is only relevant to those with low support needs, neurodivergent people have argued that this lacks a nuanced understanding of the neurodiversity movement's values (Campbell, 2020; Milton, 2019).
5. Writing about teaching disability studies as a disabled person, Campbell argues that disabled experience creates a different perspective in and on the world, but not through any epistemic privilege offered by a fictional "purity" of experience. She focuses instead on the process of subjectivity: "a complex matrix of resources of language, experience and

culture… forever in process" (p. 122). Disabled scholars are constructed as subjects, shaped by the material we are teaching or studying about ourselves, *as disabled people* – an embodied position that sometimes comes with what Campbell calls "seductive power" (p. 122), but which is disempowering in other ways, including in the vulnerability of our positionality, particularly if we are or have made ourselves visible as disabled scholars. The disabled teaching body involves a "performance of disability" (p. 125) as we teach (or, I would add, research) in critical disability studies and related fields. This process of subjectivity is what makes disabled scholars more than just the "objects" of disability research (Campbell, 2009), and why our study and research in disability theology can have a personal impact on us, as this article discusses.

6.   Miranda Fricker (2007) writes about two types of epistemic injustice – testimonial injustice, in which the stories told by members of a marginalised group are not believed, and hermeneutical injustice, in which we are not enabled to participate in the shaping of knowledge about us.

7.   Williams writes here about her exclusion from charismatic ritual, as an autistic person, but her reflections on being unable to remake herself through narrative after trauma resonate with themes of speech and knowing.

8.   Lucy and Anthony are 2 of 14 neurodivergent participants in research for my PhD and a book (Jacobs & Richardson, 2022), from a total of 45 disabled Christians in the United Kingdom. Both were initially diagnosed with Asperger Syndrome, a diagnosis which no longer exists. Their shifting terminology for themselves reflects similar shifts in the autistic community at the time they were interviewed, in 2015.

9.   Diagnostic criteria might imagine some of Lucy and Anthony's interview contributions as a "failure of normal back-and-forth communication" (Centers for Disease Control and Prevention, 2022), but their speech is different from neuronormative standards, not deficient. Longer interviews, more time spent with the data, and participant reflection (Tracy, 2010) helped us to bridge communication gaps together.

10. Rosemarie Garland-Thomson's theory of misfitting (2011) describes how society is physically designed for non-disabled people and how disabled people misfit against its normative limits.

11. I echo Krysia Waldock in this approach (2021), who writes, "I won't be listing what Autism is or what the statistics are. Being Autistic and having faith are acutely personal parts of my life; placing them into a rubric of a typical Autism essay would be highly insensitive. I am an Autistic, it is part of my identity in the same manner as being a Christian."

12. Citational practices are political (Ahmed, 2017); I primarily cite neurodivergent writers in this article.

13. In the US and UK, the vast majority of autism research funding goes to genetic and scientific research into causes and cure (Singh et al., 2009), a bias about which autistic people have expressed concerns (Pellicano et al., 2014).

14. As Milton explains it, "when autistic people and those not on the autism spectrum attempt to interact, it is both that have a problem in terms of empathising with each other: a 'double empathy problem'" (2017, p. 13); this becomes a serious problem when neurotypical framework is imposed onto an autistic person's interactions.

15. (Allison, 2019; Jacobs & Waldock, 2020). To be clear, I am not trying to diagnose a biblical character with any 'condition' here. I am retelling the story of one who sparks recognition in me; a resistant reading (Exum, 1993), in defiance of a neuronormative theological "hegemony of the average" (Hull, 2003, p. 22) which represents biblical characters solely as neurotypical.

16. (Barclay, 2008, p. 342).

17. Elsewhere I have compared the approaches of critical disability theory and pastoral theology of disability. The former is influenced by disability theory and disabled people's perspectives (Jacobs, 2018).

18. Although neurodivergent people choose different ways to describe ourselves, identity-first language – "autistic people" – is the preferred term of a majority of autistic people (Botha et al., 2023).

19. So Hills et al. write that up to half of autistic people have "severe autism" and will never develop "functional speech" (2019, pp. 2–3). But this link is not clear. Low IQ has been over-estimated in autistic people (Dawson et al., 2007); one recent study found 18% of autistic children had additional learning disabilities (Memmott, 2019 [2022]; Roman-Urrestarazu et al., 2021). Dividing autistic people by functioning labels – a poor predictor of support needs (Alvares et al., 2020) – risks obscuring our commonalities (Bowman, 2021) and the social barriers we all face, from unmet health needs and higher mortality rates to high suicidality (Pellicano et al., 2014).

20. "[S]peaking and non-speaking is not dichotomous because autistic people can move between speaking in some environments or spaces and not in others" (Botha et al., 2023, p. 870).

21. So, for example, Leidenhag writes that "attention to those we label 'disordered' forces us to interrogate our own presumptions of order" (2022); Macaskill writes "to think properly about autism brings with it a body of further blessings for the church" (2022, p. 435). Autistic people point back to a neurotypical-led church here.

22. One exception is Macaskill, who acknowledges that autistic people have been hurt by the church: "The church is not a safe place just because it is the church" (2019, p. 96). Pastoral theology has more often discussed exclusion in *society*, following Thomas Reynolds' disability studies-based theology (2008). Even so, some theologians express unease with concepts from disability theory, such as ableism (Brock, 2022; Swinton, 2011).

23. This is in the context of an "empirical turn" towards theological ethnography (Kaufman, 2015; Marti, 2016).

24. "Nothing about us, without us" is a maxim of the disability and neurodiversity movements (Silberman, 2015).

25. Not all neurodivergent people consider themselves disabled. However, the neurodiversity paradigm is a social model, showing how we are disabled by barriers in a neuronormative society (Walker, 2021).

26. The same pastoral model of disability frames theological approaches to neurodivergent people and disabled people more generally (Jacobs, 2018).

27. These are not uncontested stories. Brock writes, "The practice of telling stories to establish the moral authority of the speaker... needlessly narrows the discussion and excludes important voices" (2019, p. 242). Rosemarie Garland-Thomson (1997) would agree that stories told by non-disabled people to legitimize their right to speak about disabled people are problematic. However, obscuring the difference in positionality between stories *about us* and disabled and neurodivergent people's *own* untold stories of our marginalisation can reinscribe the silencing of disabled and neurodivergent voices in theology (Jacobs, 2018).

28. There is very little theology engaging with ADHD (Barclay, 2008) and almost nothing on Tourette's Syndrome – one exception is Beers (2020).

29. In their research on autistic sociality, Rosqvist et al. argue that "we need to explore alternative possibilities for understanding friendships, ones that do not necessarily include the dominant NT ideals of researchers" (2015).

30. Anthony did significant emotion work here to compensate for the double empathy problem. Neurodivergent people are often known – and sometimes pathologized –

for our strong sense of justice, in defiance of the idea that we lack theory of mind (Russell et al., 2019; Schäfer & Kraneburg, 2015).
31. We all need "the right to participate in the 'living tradition' or the reflexive arguments" of a society or institution (May, 2011, p. 368; Shotter, 1993).
32. However, testimony is "mere 'story-telling'" (Stone & Priestley, 1996, p. 20) without theory about the social conditions and inequalities that produce the situated knowledges of marginalized groups (see also Radford, 2022).
33. Participants in my research critiqued theologies that fail to speak out against harmful approaches to disability, neurodiversity and distress, offering only "lightweight" responses (Jacobs, 2018, p. 215).
34. "Grudgingly opening the door a little bit is not enough," writes Nicola Martin (2020), identifying neurotypical privilege in an academy that needs to "accommodate a widening range of approaches and thinking styles."
35. For example, in 2019, the annual 'Living Edge' conference on disability and church was themed 'Thinking Differently About God.' Neurodivergent people reflected theologically from lived experience of autism, dyslexia, psychosis, learning disability and more, on church, the Bible and faith (Allison, 2019; Hartley, 2019).
36. (Williams, 2022, p. 195).
37. (Williams, 2022, p. 200).
38. (Williams, 2022, p. 199).
39. Adapted from *Safety In Numbers: Autism, Theology and Me* (Jacobs, 2022).

Acknowledgements

The author would like to thank Krysia Waldock and Fiona MacMillan for advice on an early version of the manuscript.

Ethics statement

The primary data cited in this article comes from a PhD study which received ethical approval from the Department of Sociology, University of Sheffield and the Department of the Study of Religions, SOAS, University of London.

Funding

No funding was received for this article. The article draws on data from a PhD study which was supported by the St Luke's College Foundation under grant number 011J-13 and Funds for Women Graduates.

ORCID

Naomi Lawson Jacobs http://orcid.org/0000-0001-8052-9403

References

Ahmed, S. (2000). Who knows? Knowing strangers and strangerness. *Australian Feminist Studies, 15*(31), 49–68. https://doi.org/10.1080/713611918
Ahmed, S. (2017). *Living a feminist life*. Duke University Press.

Allison, B. (2019, 12–13 October). *Thinking Differently About the Bible*. Thinking differently about god: Neurodiversity, Faith and Church, St Martin-in-the-Fields Church, London. https://www.inclusive-church.org/disability-conferences/.

Allison, B. (2021). *Shut in, shut out, shut up: Neurodiversity and Church: Intersectionality* [Video]. HeartEdge. https://youtu.be/SI-AP29onrw.

Alvares, G. A., Bebbington, K., Cleary, D., Evans, K., Glasson, E. J., Maybery, M. T., Pillar, S., Uljarević, M., Varcin, K., Wray, J., & Whitehouse, A. J. (2020). The misnomer of 'high functioning autism': Intelligence is an imprecise predictor of functional abilities at diagnosis. *Autism, 24*(1), 221–232. https://doi.org/10.1177/1362361319852831

Barclay, A. (2008). Does Peter have Attention Deficit Hyperactivity Disorder (ADHD)? *Journal of Religion, Disability & Health, 12*(4), 330–346. https://doi.org/10.1080/15228960802515634

Baron-Cohen, S. (1997). *Mindblindness: An essay on autism and theory of mind*. MIT Press.

Beers, J. (2020). *A video resource for teaching meditative prayer in the Christian Tradition to people living with tourette syndrome* [D.Min. diss.]. Ashland Theological Seminary. http://rave.ohiolink.edu/etdc/view?acc_num=atssem1608643878170021.

Belser, J. W. (2019). *God on wheels: Disability liberation and spiritual leadership* [Video]. Yale Divinity School. www.youtube.com/watch?v=tjq7sWgwsQk.

Betcher, S. V. (2007). *Spirit and the politics of disablement*. Fortress Press.

Boot, M. (2022). Review: Autistic thinking in the life of the Church by Stewart Rapley. *Church Times*. https://www.churchtimes.co.uk/articles/2022/18-february/books-arts/book-reviews/autistic-thinking-in-the-life-of-the-church-by-stewart-rapley.

Botha, M., & Cage, E. (2022). "Autism research is in crisis": A mixed method study of researchers' constructions of autistic people and autism research. *Frontiers in Psychology, 13*(1), 1050897. https://doi.org/10.3389/fpsyg.2022.1050897

Botha, M., Hanlon, J., & Williams, G. L. (2023). Does language matter? Identity-first versus person-first language use in autism research: A response to Vivanti. *Journal of Autism and Developmental Disorders, 53*(2), 870–878. https://doi.org/10.1007/s10803-020-04858-w

Bowman, D. (2021). *On the spectrum: Autism, faith, and the gifts of neurodiversity* (Kindle ed.). Brazos Press.

Brock, B. (2009). Autism, care, and christian hope. *Journal of Religion, Disability & Health, 13*(1), 7–28. https://doi.org/10.1080/15228960802581404

Brock, B. (2019). *Wondrously wounded: Theology, disability, and the body of Christ*. Baylor University Press.

Brock, B. (2022). On the limits of justice as eradicating 'Isms'. *International Journal for the Study of the Christian Church, 22*(1), 75–85. https://doi.org/10.1080/1474225X.2022.2038017

Brown, N., & Leigh, J. (Eds.) (2020). *Ableism in academia: Theorising experiences of disabilities and chronic iilnesses in higher education* (eBook ed.). UCL Press.

Bumiller, K. (2008). Quirky citizens: Autism, gender, and reimagining disability. *Journal of Women in Culture and Society, 33*(4), 967–991. https://doi.org/10.1086/528848

Burnett, E. R. (2021). "Different, not less": Pastoral care of autistic adults within Christian Churches. *Practical Theology, 14*(3), 211–223. https://doi.org/10.1080/1756073X.2020.1850402

Bustion, O. (2017). Autism and christianity: An ethnographic intervention. *Journal of the American Academy of Religion, 85*(3), lfw075. https://doi.org/10.1093/jaarel/lfw075

Campbell, F. K. (2009). *Contours of ableism: The production of disability and abledness*. Palgrave Macmillan.

Campbell, M. (2020). Neurodiversity: Not just about autism! In D. Milton (Ed.), *The neurodiversity reader: Exploring concepts, lived experience and implications for practice* (pp. 67–76). Pavilion Publishing.

Centers for Disease Control and Prevention. (2022). *Autism Spectrum Disorder (ASD): Diagnostic Criteria*. U.S. Department of Health & Human Services. Retrieved April 2, 2023, from https://www.cdc.gov/ncbddd/autism/hcp-dsm.html.

Chapman, R., & Botha, M. (2023). Neurodivergence-informed therapy. *Developmental Medicine and Child Neurology*, 65(3), 310–317. https://doi.org/10.1111/dmcn.15384

Chapman, R., & Carel, H. (2022). Neurodiversity, epistemic injustice, and the good human life. *Journal of Social Philosophy*, 53(4), 614–631. https://doi.org/10.1111/josp.12456

Chopp, R. S. (1987). Practical theology and liberation. In L. S. Mudge & J. N. Poling (Eds.), *Formation and reflection: The promise of practical theology*. Fortress Press.

Cone, J. (1975). *God of the oppressed*. Harper Collins.

Cox, J. A. (2017). *Autism, humanity and personhood: A christ-centred theological anthropology* (eBook ed.). Cambridge Scholars Publishing.

Crowder, K. (2022). Talking through autism: Auto-ethnographic reflections on participating in UK Autism support groups. In K. L. Aldred, P. Daly, T. Albanna, & T. Hendren (Eds.), *Rainbow goddess: Celebrating neurodiversity* (Kindle ed., pp. 65–71). Girl God Books.

Davis, L. J. (1995). *Enforcing normalcy: Disability, deafness, and the body*. Verso.

Dawson, M., Soulières, I., Gernsbacher, M. A., & Mottron, L. (2007). The level and nature of autistic intelligence. *Psychological Science*, 18(8), 657–662. https://doi.org/10.1111/j.1467-9280.2007.01954.x

Dearey, P. (2009). Do the autistic have a prayer? *Journal of Religion, Disability & Health*, 13(1), 40–50. https://doi.org/10.1080/15228960802581420

Deeley, Q. (2009). Cognitive style, spirituality, and religious understanding: The case of autism. *Journal of Religion, Disability & Health*, 13(1), 77–82. https://doi.org/10.1080/15228960802581479

Deligny, F. (2015). *The Arachnean and other texts*. University of Minnesota Press.

Denzin, N. (2014). *Interpretive autoethnography* (2nd ed.). SAGE Publications.

Dubin, N., & Graetz, J. E. (2009). Through a different lens: Spirituality in the lives of individuals with Asperger's Syndrome. *Journal of Religion, Disability & Health*, 13(1), 29–39. https://doi.org/10.1080/15228960802505213

Edmonds, M. (2011). *A theological diagnosis: A new direction on genetic therapy, 'disability' and the ethics of healing*. Jessica Kingsley.

Eiesland, N. L. (1994). *The disabled god: Toward a liberatory theology of disability*. Abingdon Press.

Evers, D. (2017). Neurodiversity, normality, and theological anthropology. *Philosophy, Theology and the Sciences*, 4(2), 160. https://doi.org/10.1628/ptsc-2017-0004

Exum, J. C. (1993). *Fragmented women: Feminist (Sub)versions of biblical narratives*. Trinity Press.

Fricker, M. (2007). *Epistemic injustice: Power and the ethics of knowing*. Oxford University Press.

Frith, U. (2008). *Autism: A very short introduction*. Oxford University Press.

Garland-Thomson, R. (1997). *Extraordinary bodies: Figuring disability in American culture and literature*. Columbia University Press.

Garland-Thomson, R. (2011). Misfits: A feminist materialist disability concept. *Hypatia*, 26(3), 591–609. https://doi.org/10.1111/j.1527-2001.2011.01206.x

Gillibrand, J. (2014). *Disabled Church – Disabled society: The implications of autism for philosophy, theology and politics*. Jessica Kingsley.

Gordon, J. (2009). Is a sense of self essential to spirituality? *Journal of Religion, Disability & Health*, *13*(1), 51–63. https://doi.org/10.1080/15228960802581438

Graby, S. (2015). Neurodiversity: Bridging the gap between the disabled people's movement and the mental health system survivors' movement? In H. Spandler, J. Anderson, & B. Sapey (Eds.), *Madness, distress and the politics of disablement* (pp. 231–244). Policy Press.

Hardwick, L. (2021). *Disabiity and the Church: A vision for diversity and inclusion* (Kindle ed.). InterVarsity Press.

Harshaw, J. (2012). Autism and love: Learning what love looks like – A response. *Practical Theology*, *5*(3), 279–286. https://doi.org/10.1558/prth.v5i3.279

Hartley, S. (2019, 12–13 October). *Ignatian perspectives on neurodiversity*. Thinking differently about god: Neurodiversity, faith and Church, St Martin-in-the-Fields Church, London. https://www.inclusive-church.org/disability-conferences/.

Hauerwas, S. (2013). *Approaching the end: Eschatological reflections on church, politics, and life*. William B. Eerdmans Publishing.

Hills, K., Clapton, J., & Dorsett, P. (2019). Spirituality in the context of nonverbal autism: Practical and theological considerations. *Practical Theology*, *12*(2), 186–197. https://doi.org/10.1080/1756073X.2019.1592927

Huijg, D. D. (2020). Neuronormativity in theorising agency: An argument for a critical neurodiversity approach. In H. B. Rosqvist, N. Chown, & A. Stenning (Eds.), *Neurodiversity studies: A new critical paradigm* (eBook ed., pp. 213–217). Routledge.

Hull, J. M. (2003). A spirituality of disability: The Christian Heritage as both problem and potential. *Studies in Christian Ethics*, *16*(2), 21–35. https://doi.org/10.1177/095394680301600202

Hull, J. M. (2014). Theology of disability. In Inclusive Church (Ed.), *Disability: The Inclusive Church Resource* (Kindle ed.) Darton, Longman and Todd Ltd.

Jacobs, N. L. (2018). *The upside-down kingdom of God: A disability studies perspective on disabled people's experiences in Churches and theologies of disability*. [Ph.D. diss., SOAS]. University of London.

Jacobs, N. L. (2022, February 2023). Safety in numbers: Autism, theology and me. Blog. *At the Gates*. https://naomilawsonjacobs.com/safety-in-numbers-autism-theology-and-me/.

Jacobs, N. L., & Richardson, E. (2022). *At the gates: Disability, justice and the Churches*. Darton, Longman and Todd Ltd.

Jacobs, N. L., Waldock, K. (2020). *Shut in, shut out, shut up: Disability, social justice and the Church* [Video]. HeartEdge. https://www.facebook.com/watch/?v=131192265202436.

Kafer, A. (2013). *Feminist, Queer, Crip*. University of Indiana Press.

Kaufman, T. S. (2015). Normativity as pitfall or Ally?: Reflexivity as an interpretive resource in ecclesiological and ethnographic research. *Ecclesial Practices*, *2*(1), 91–107. https://doi.org/10.1163/22144471-00201006

Kenny, A. (2022). *My body is not a prayer request* (Kindle ed.). Brazos Press.

Leidenhag, J. (2021). The challenge of autism for relational approaches to theological anthropology. *International Journal of Systematic Theology*, *23*(1), 109–134. https://doi.org/10.1111/ijst.12453

Leidenhag, J. (2022). Psychological disorders and the divine order: Towards a science-engaged theology of autism. In B. Sollereder & A. McGrath (Eds.), *Emerging voices in science and theology: Contributions by young women* (eBook ed.). Routledge.

Lewis, A. (2009). Methodological issues in exploring the ideas of children with autism concerning self and spirituality. *Journal of Religion, Disability & Health*, *13*(1), 64–76. https://doi.org/10.1080/15228960802581446

Lewis, H. (2007). *Deaf liberation theology*. Ashgate Publishing.

Luterman, S. (2019). The trials of being autistic at an autism research conference. *Undark*. https://undark.org/2019/07/11/being-autistic-at-an-autism-research-conference/.

Macaskill, G. (2019). *Autism and the Church: Bible, theology, and community* (Kindle ed.). Baylor University Press.

Macaskill, G. (2022). The bible, autism and other profound developmental conditions: Regulating hermeneutics. *Journal of Disability & Religion*, *26*(4), 414–438. https://doi.org/10.1080/23312521.2021.1881024

Marti, G. (2016). Found theologies versus imposed theologies: Remarks on theology and ethnography from a sociological perspective. *Ecclesial Practices*, *3*(2), 157–172. https://doi.org/10.1163/22144471-00302002

Martin, N. (2020). Practical scholarship: Optimising beneficial research collaborations between autistic scholars, professional services staff, and 'typical academics' in UK Universities. In H. B. Rosqvist, N. Chown, & A. Stenning (Eds.), *Neurodiversity studies: A new critical paradigm* (eBook ed.). Routledge.

May, V. (2011). Self, belonging and social change. *Sociology*, *45*(3), 363–378. https://doi.org/10.1177/0038038511399624

Memmott, A. (2019). *Welcoming and including autistic people in our churches and communities*. Diocese of Oxford. https://churchesforall.org.uk/wp-content/uploads/2019/12/Autism-Guidelines-2019-Oxford-Diocese.pdf.

Memmott, A. (2019 [2022], February 2023). Autism and IQ. *Ann's Autism Blog*. http://annsautism.blogspot.com/2019/09/autism-and-iq-oh-my-we-had-this-one.html.

Memmott, A., Noël, R. (2020). *Shut in, shut out, shut up: Neurodiversity and Church* [Video]. HeartEdge. https://www.youtube.com/watch?v=uDLFudfvOLk.

Michalko, R. (2002). *The difference that disability makes*. Temple University Press.

Milton, D. (2017). *A mismatch of salience: Exploration of the nature of autism from theory to practice*. Pavilion Publishing.

Milton, D. (2019). Disagreeing over neurodiversity. *Psychologist*, *32*, 8. https://www.bps.org.uk/psychologist/disagreeing-over-neurodiversity.

Milton, D. (2020). Neurodiversity past and present: An introduction to the neurodiversity reader. In D. Milton (Ed.), *The neurodiversity reader: Exploring concepts, lived experience and implications for practice* (pp. 3–6). Pavilion Publishing.

Milton, D., & Bracher, M. (2013). Autistics speak but are they heard? *Medical Sociology Online*, *7*(2), 61–69. https://kar.kent.ac.uk/62635/.

Morgan, H. R. (2022). Autism and purity culture. *Canadian Journal of Theology, Mental Health and Disability*, *2*(2), 39544. https://jps.library.utoronto.ca/index.php/cjtmhd/article/view/39544.

Mueller, L. (2020). From neuronormativity to neurodiversity: Changing perspectives on autism. In D. Milton (Ed.), *The neurodiversity reader: Exploring concepts, lived experience and implications for practice* (pp. 94–104). Pavilion Publishing.

Muers, R., & Grant, R. (2017). Theology at thresholds: Learning from a practice in transition. *Ecclesial Practices*, *4*(1), 45–62. https://doi.org/10.1163/22144471-00401005

Murray, D., Lesser, M., & Lawson, W. (2005). Attention, monotropism and the diagnostic criteria for Autism. *The International Journal of Research and Practice*, *9*(2), 139–156. https://doi.org/10.1177/1362361305051398

Noël, R., & MacMillan, F. (2022). Theology at the borders of psychosis: Transcendence of the artificial borders of sanity, ableism and the implications for practical ministry. *Anvil Journal of Theology and Mission*, *38*(1). https://churchmissionsociety.org/anvil/theology-at-the-borders-of-psychosis-rachel-noel-fiona-macmillan-anvil-vol-38-issue-1/.

O'Dell, L., Rosqvist, H. B., Ortega, F., Brownlow, C., & Orsini, M. (2016). Critical autism studies: Exploring epistemic dialogues and intersections, challenging dominant understandings of autism. *Disability & Society, 31*(2), 166–179. https://doi.org/10.1080/0968 7599.2016.1164026

Pellicano, E., Adam, D., & Charman, T. (2014). What should autism research focus upon? Community views and priorities from the United Kingdom. *Autism, 18*(7), 756–770. https://doi.org/10.1177/1362361314529627

Pitard, J. (2017). A journey to the centre of self: Positioning the researcher in autoethnography. *Forum Qualitative Sozialforschung/Forum, 18*(3), 2764. https://doi.org/10.17169/fqs-18.3.2764

Radford, C. W. (2022). *Lived experiences and social transformations: Poetics, politics and power relations in practical theology.* Brill.

Raffety, E. (2020). From depression and decline to repentance and transformation: Receiving disabled leadership and its gifts for the Church. *Theology Today, 77*(2), 117–123. https://doi.org/10.1177/0040573620924558

Raffety, E. (2021). Listening even unto rebuke. *Canadian Journal of Theology, Mental Health and Disability, 1*(2), 117–121. https://jps.library.utoronto.ca/index.php/cjtmhd/article/view/37800/28760

Raffety, E. (2022). *From inclusion to justice: Disability, ministry, and congregational leadership.* Baylor University Press.

Rapley, S. (2021). *Autistic thinking in the life of the Church.* SCM Press.

Reynolds, T. E. (2008). *Vulnerable communion: A theology of disability and hospitality.* Brazos Press.

Richardson, E., Jacobs, N. L., MacMillan, F. (2022). *Book launch: At the Gates: Disability, Justice and the Churches* [Video]. https://youtu.be/Ib047-GsJPk.

Roman-Urrestarazu, A., van Kessel, R., Allison, C., Matthews, F. E., Brayne, C., & Baron-Cohen, S. (2021). Association of race/ethnicity and social disadvantage with autism prevalence in 7 Million school children in England. *JAMA Pediatrics, 175*(6), e210054. https://jamanetwork.com/journals/jamapediatrics/fullarticle/2777821 https://doi.org/10.1001/jamapediatrics.2021.0054

Bertilsdotter Rosqvist, H., Brownlow, C., & ÓDell, L. (2015). "What's the point of having friends?": Reformulating notions of the meaning of friends and friendship among autistic people. *Disability Studies Quarterly, 35*(4), 4109. https://dsq-sds.org/article/view/3254/4109 https://doi.org/10.18061/dsq.v35i4.3254

Russell, G., Kapp, S. K., Elliott, D., Elphick, C., Gwernan-Jones, R., & Owens, C. (2019). mapping the autistic advantage from the accounts of adults diagnosed with autism: A qualitative study. *Autism in Adulthood, 1*(2), 124–133. https://doi.org/10.1089/aut.2018.0035

Schäfer, T., & Kraneburg, T. (2015). The kind nature behind the unsocial semblance: ADHD and justice sensitivity – A pilot study. *Journal of Attention Disorders, 19*(8), 715–727. https://doi.org/10.1177/1087054712466914

Shotter, J. (1993). *Cultural politics of everyday life.* Open University Press.

Shrier, P. (2018). Messengers of hope: A boy with autism, his Church, and the special olympics. In N. J. Watson, K. Hargaden, & B. Brock (Eds.), *Theology, disability and sport: Social justice perspectives* (eBook ed.). Routledge.

Silberman, S. (2015). *Neurotribes: The legacy of autism and the future of neurodiversity* (eBook ed.). Penguin Random House.

Singer, J. (2016). *Neurodiversity: The birth of an idea* (Kindle ed.). Lexington: Judy Singer.

Singh, J., Illes, J., Lazzeroni, L., & Hallmayer, J. (2009). Trends in US autism research funding. *Journal of Autism and Developmental Disorders, 39*(5), 788–795. https://doi.org/10.1007/s10803-008-0685-0

Spies, M. (2021). From belonging as Supercrip to Misfitting as Crip: Journeying through seminary. *Journal of Disability & Religion*, *25*(3), 296–311. https://doi.org/10.1080/233 12521.2021.1895028

Stone, E., & Priestley, M. (1996). Parasites, pawns and partners: Disability research and the role of non-disabled researchers. *The British Journal of Sociology*, *47*(4), 699–716. https://eprints.whiterose.ac.uk/927/ https://doi.org/10.2307/591081

Swinton, J. (2011). Who is the god we worship? Theologies of disability; challenges and new possibilities. *International Journal of Practical Theology*, *14*(2), 273–307. https://doi. org/10.1515/ijpt.2011.020

Swinton, J. (2012). Reflections on autistic love: What does love look like? *Practical Theology*, *5*(3), 259–278. https://doi.org/10.1558/prth.v5i3.259

Swinton, J., & Trevett, C. (2009). Religion and autism: Initiating an interdisciplinary conversation. *Journal of Religion, Disability & Health*, *13*(1), 2–6. https://doi. org/10.1080/15228960802606193

Tam, C. (2021). *Kinship in the household of god: Towards a practical theology of belonging and spiritual care of people with profound autism*. Wipf and Stock Publishers.

Tam, C. (2022). Faithful presence: A practice of belonging with people experiencing profound autism. *International Journal for the Study of the Christian Church*, *22*(1), 21–34. https://doi.org/10.1080/1474225X.2022.2035580

Tracy, S. J. (2010). Qualitative quality: Eight "big-tent" criteria for excellent qualitative research. *Qualitative Inquiry*, *16*(10), 837–851. https://doi.org/10.1177/1077800410383121

van Ommen, A. L., & Endress, T. (2022). Reframing liturgical theology through the lens of autism: A Qualitative study of autistic experiences of worship. *Studia Liturgica*, *52*(2), 219–234. https://doi.org/10.1177/00393207221111573

Waldock, K. (2021). "Doing Church" during COVID-19: An autistic reflection on online Church. *Canadian Journal of Theology, Mental Health and Disability*, *1*(1), 34930. https://jps.library.utoronto.ca/index.php/cjtmhd/article/view/34930.

Waldock, K. (2023, 13–14 March). *Conceptualising belonging: The views of autistic people* [Paper presentation]. ITAKOM Conference, Edinburgh [Poster presentation].

Waldock, K., & Forrester-Jones, R. (2020). An exploratory study of attitudes toward autism amongst church-going Christians in the South East of England, United Kingdom. *Journal of Disability & Religion*, *24*(4), 349–370. https://doi.org/10.1080/23312521.2020.1776667

Walker, N. (2021). *Neuroqueer heresies: Notes on the neurodiversity paradigm, autistic empowerment, and postnormal possibilities* (Kindle ed.). Autonomous Press.

Williams, C. (2022). Autism: An autoethnography of a peculiar trauma. In K. O'Donnell & K. Cross (Eds.), *Bearing witness: Intersectional perspectives on trauma theology* (pp. 187–204). SCM Press.

Yergeau, M. (2013). Clinically significant disturbance: On theorists who theorize theory of mind. *Disability Studies Quarterly*, *33*(4), 3876. https://doi.org/10.18061/dsq.v33i4

🔓 OPEN ACCESS

The Impossible Subject: Belonging as a Neurodivergent in Congregations

Krysia Emily Waldock (iD)

ABSTRACT
Neurodivergent people have been reported in academic literature to not always feel a sense of belonging within church congregations. Previous scholarship has highlighted that some neurodivergent people may be stigmatized and/or excluded within congregational settings. However little attention has been paid to how neurodivergent people belong within congregations, especially from a neurodivergent perspective. Using an autoethnographic methodology, I interrogate my own personal narrative of belonging within congregational spaces. I blended Goffman's social stigma theory and Scambler's theorization of social stigma to examine a neurodivergent experience within church congregations, and to explore the interface between being neurodivergent and feeling a sense of belonging in a church congregation. This autoethnography highlights how impression management (particularly passing and masking) are central to the feelings of belonging, and lack of belonging, I experienced. How church is "done" also appears to influence feelings of belonging, with norms in the churches mentioned in the narrative often shaped by normalcy.

Introduction

> I wasn't gently placed on the margins, I questioned and struggled being placed there.
> (Waldock, 2021)

Scholars have argued that both theological reflection (van Ommen, 2022a; van Ommen & Endress, 2022) and social scientific inquiry (Waldock & Sango, 2023) focusing on autism and church is a recent phenomenon. There is also a lack of papers in this field informed by the neurodiversity paradigm. The central aim of this paper is to present an autoethnographic account of belonging in church congregations from a neurodivergent perspective. As an openly Autistic and disabled scholar, I firmly believe that marginalized voices within discourses can unveil both further directions

This is an Open Access article distributed under the terms of the Creative Commons Attribution-NonCommercial License (http://creativecommons.org/licenses/by-nc/4.0/), which permits unrestricted non-commercial use, distribution, and reproduction in any medium, provided the original work is properly cited. The terms on which this article has been published allow the posting of the Accepted Manuscript in a repository by the author(s) or with their consent.

for research and inquiry, but also present us with theological ponderings to further deepen our understanding of the disabled God (Eiesland, 1994). The research question framing this study is: What is the interface between being neurodivergent and feeling a sense of belonging in a Church congregation?

The means in which I present my narrative is inspired by both Javaid (2020) and Spies (2021). I used both pieces as seminar texts for my first-year undergraduate students in Religion, Philosophy and Ethics to introduce the concept of social stigma within religious contexts and cultures for people with marginalized and oppressed identities. To date, a lack of work has been undertaken on the interface of neurodivergent identity and belonging within religious contexts, and the impact of a religious context upon how neurodivergent people perceive themselves. Past work has emphasized the importance of neurodivergent identity as a lens to understand church contexts (Jacobs, 2022; Waldock, 2021). The social and cultural experience of being neurodivergent within congregational contexts is unique from other social groups (such as sports groups) due to the theology that underpins the purpose of gathering and in some ways, unites congregants. Insider knowledge of this cultural landscape through a neurodivergent lived experience lens can shed more light on the lived reality of being neurodivergent within congregations, and how belonging is experienced.

I will use both Goffman's (1963) social stigma theory and Scambler's (2004) reframing of stigma through differentiation between felt and enacted stigma as lenses to observe and understand how my neurodivergent body, brain and identity interact with other congregants. Despite churchgoers all being one in Christ (Romans 12:5), prejudicial attitudes have been discovered within churches in relation to autism, with Autistic bodies and brains being stigmatized (Waldock & Forrester-Jones, 2020). How disabled people (including neurodivergent people) have been viewed and understood by the church has changed over time, ranging from witchcraft (Kramer & Sprenger, 1928/1971, p. 45), a blessing (Frith, 2003, p. 22), the devil (Miles, 2001) or a gift (Moltmann, 1998, p. 120). Goffman further supports the theoretical framing of prejudicial attitudes by arguing that individuals without a stigma[1] perceive individuals with a stigma as "not quite human" (1963, p. 15). In this manner, neurodivergent bodies and brains are problematized through stigma being an ontological deficit (Scambler, 2009). Social stigma theory is an appropriate lens through which to further explore belonging, as Goffman (1963) defines stigma as "an attribute that is deeply discrediting" (p. 13) and disqualifies the individual from full social acceptance (p. 19). Social acceptance has been reported by some neurodivergent people as central to feelings of belonging using focus groups (Waldock et al., 2021), but also more broadly in the wider neurodiverse population (Leary, 2010; Pardede et al., 2020). Specifically within a congregational context, Carter and colleagues (2016) outline acceptance as one of their ten dimensions to belonging for Autistic people and people with an intellectual disability under the broader field of "relational depth."

One further aspect that strengthens social stigma theory as a framework to understand neurodivergent belonging in congregations is the importance placed on interaction and relationships. Goffman (1963, p. 24) himself focuses on what he calls "mixed contacts" (contact and interaction between someone who is not stigmatized and someone who is stigmatized). Compensation strategies employed by those who are stigmatized, such as passing and masking, occur within social environments and relationships (Miller et al., 2021; Radulski, 2022). A variety of studies have focused on how neurodivergent people (in particular Autistic people; Sedgewick et al., 2021) may utilize masking and passing to navigate having a "discreditable"[2] identity and gain social acceptance. Church congregations are composed of people and therefore inherently based upon a social setting, and interpersonal contact and relationships. In addition, Scambler (2004) differentiates between felt and enacted stigma. Scambler (2009) defines felt stigma as the sense of shame and fear of experiencing enacted stigma, whilst enacted stigma refers to overt discrimination based on recognition of a stigmatized identity. Felt and enacted stigma are of particular importance in understanding both my own account of belonging as a neurodivergent person, and more broadly, as belonging is is not necessarily externally visible.

Belonging in churches

Language in relation to belonging in congregations, alike within the academic literature, can be imprecise and nebulous. Particular focus in this case is given to the frequent usage of "welcome" within congregations by church leadership to refer to aspects of belonging and inclusion. I notably differentiate between belonging and welcome, without proper interrogation of exactly how similar, or dissimilar they are, further imprecision of terms can occur. Ann Memmott argues for a differentiation of the two terms, with belong seen as somewhat stronger than welcome as she states:

Notice the word I used.

Belong.

Not 'welcome'.

Belong. (Memmott, 2019)

Memmott's (2019) assertion identifies belonging as bidirectional and intersubjective (echoing Mahar et al., 2013) rather than a performance of welcome, which could be interpreted in some contexts. Carter and colleagues (2016) also differentiate between "welcome" and "belonging," with "welcome" as one subdomain within the broader concept of belonging and other elements such as befriending and acceptance necessary for belonging to occur. Carter and colleagues (2016) also differentiate between being present and having a presence (i.e., interactional depth, friendship) within a congregation for Autistic people and people with an intellectual disability. In spaces where I have been able to come as I am and valued within, not merely welcomed, placated and expected to meet norms, authentic feelings of belonging have developed.

Biblical exploration of belonging emphasizes the bidirectional and intersubjective nature of belonging, going beyond notions of "welcome." A relational dynamic with humans belonging to God is present (Isaiah 44:5; Psalm 100:3; Romans 14:8) and more specifically the body of Christ (Galatians 3:28; Romans 12:5). Furthermore humankind has been described as being made "all in God's image" (Genesis 1:27), illustrating the relational dynamic between humanity and God, and this is furthered with "for where two or three gather in my name, there am I with them" (Matthew 18:20). In this light, some may perhaps argue belonging to be at the center of Christian teachings, both in relation to how humankind is one with God, and however we may gather, God is described to be with us. These ideas demonstrate conflict between Biblical discussion and the language churches use, and therefore how we "do church."

Methods

Autoethnographers have argued that writing helps us make sense of the world and the events that happen to us (Ellis et al., 2011). Therefore a sensemaking exercise is deeply entangled with who I am as a researcher, who I am as a person and the lenses through which I see things. By using my own story as an Autistic person who used to attend church, I hope to be able to illuminate an experience of being neurodivergent within a congregation. I will pay particular attention to the "coming out" of my neurodivergent identity within a congregational space when I attended churches in person. It also impacts and shapes the social research I do, and the research questions I ask (Holman Jones, 2016).

Data generation and analysis

After refining my research question and theoretical framework in November 2021, I started collecting memories of my own experiences within churches throughout my life. As someone who attended church regularly until a few years ago, this meant capturing as much as I could remember throughout my churchgoing experiences. It is understood that memories are perhaps viewed with suspicion in regards to their objectivity and reality, however this paper is interested in how I make sense of my lived experience (Bochner & Ellis, 2016). Through capturing memories, I allowed all memories to be noted so I could be intentional with what to highlight within my analysis (Cooper & Lilyea, 2022) and compose my story, given storymaking has been described as composition (Bochner, 2017, p. 74).

During March and April 2023, I familiarized myself with my story, then 'smoothed' it by placing it in chronological order and removing repetitions where they existed. Next I considered the overall plot and any mini stories and plots within the main story, notably the story that occurred within each church. I sought the critical incidents within the larger story and within each mini story, and compared them. This allowed me to see if there were indeed any similarities or differences within the turning points of my story. I then focused on these critical incidents and considered them in light of both Goffman's and Scambler's theoretical frameworks. I "zoomed in and out" (as described by Anderson, 2020) to explore and recognize links between my story and the broader cultural context, both within churches, and of neurodivergent people (Chang, 2008).

Ethical considerations

Being an Autistic and disabled scholar, these are experiences I use to help me make sense of the world around me. Being Autistic is a lens I see the world through—it is inextricable from who I am. As being Autistic is a "developmental phenomenon" (Walker, 2021), I have never known any other perspective or existence, even if I was not aware of exactly "what" this perspective is. My theological standpoint is also a significant consideration both within my positionality and my ongoing reflexivity. I hold beliefs in line with liberation theology (Gutiérrez, 1973). I view all of humanity as made in God's own image (Genesis, 1:27) and diversity as necessary (Galatians, 3:28). Being reflexive allows the lenses and perspectives my data filtered through to be made clear. Being Autistic for me is not a negative thing, however I do not subscribe to the "Autism as superpower" narrative, nor that being Autistic is a gift. It just is—a neutral identifier with connotations embroiled in stigma and othering due to societal attitudes and structures. The beliefs I hold frame how I understand and view other people within and outside of congregations, seeing everyone as having inherent value. Bringing these lenses to redescribe my story means the story I tell is not the same perhaps as it happened (Bochner, 2017), or as others would tell it. As Bochner (2017) argues, 'my memory of events is my memory now; it is what I remember now, not what I knew then' (p. 73).

Throughout the writing of this paper, I confronted many times feelings of unease and discomfort. Am I disclosing too much? Am I comfortable sharing what I am sharing? Is this a story that should be told? As Ellis (2007) states, this question is often one that underpins personal narratives. Questions in previous autoethnographic studies have raised this possibility, including harm to career trajectory (Rambo, 2016). I made the decision that this is a story to share, given its topicality. I am in a position of privilege and power within academia that I can access means of disseminating scholarly works, and that my voice could be taken more seriously than my practitioner and nonacademic colleagues. Although I could risk being a "self-narrating zoo exhibit" in the words of Jim Sinclair (Waltz, 2013), I believe through the power I hold that the neurodivergent voice needs to be added to conversations on belonging in congregations, which is seldom sought. I am acutely aware that not all disabled and neurodivergent people in churches may have had the same experience as me (for example, Spies, 2021; van Ommen & Endress, 2022). There appears to be no grand narrative in relation to how neurodivergent people navigate church congregations.

I am additionally aware that others are embroiled into my narrative through having been in my life during the times I am narrating. Their views and opinions are presented from my own positionality as a marginalized Autistic and disabled person, and their views and opinions may have changed since their place within my story. Even though within a congregational space (and many other non-autistic majority spaces) I am disempowered, within a research space I am perceived as having power through the titles I hold (PhD Candidate, Research Assistant) and the that I am in control of how the narrative is presented in this paper. This "fragmented self" (Ellis, 2007) is to be navigated carefully. As part of relational ethics (Ellis, 2007), it is important to consider how others are presented as their own experience or narrative may differ (see Edwards, 2021) and notably to stay aware of individuals' views who may well be different due to cultural or gender difference (Etherington, 2007). Therefore the following steps have been taken to take account for relational ethics: (1) the congregations I refer to, and individuals have been anonymised; (2) composite characters (blending the characteristics of individuals together) have been used where an interaction is the focus within the plot of my narrative; and (3) a fellow congregant read the story to ensure that "the dust and clutter is shown without saying they're dirty" (Ellis, 2007, p. 25). These three steps assist navigating the ethical dilemmas in how I represent other actors in my story.

My story

When I did not know, nor accept, I was neurodivergent

My story starts in Church A[3]. I attended this church for many years throughout my childhood and teenage years, noticing I was "different" before I knew what being neurodivergent meant. The world was loud, bright and busy, but I believed everyone was just better at managing this than I was. I grew up in this church from a young age. My memory is more fragmented in my younger years, but I do have certain distinct and clear memories, one being singing in church with my dad aged 3 in the middle front rows using the small A6 blue hymn books. The books had that distinct hymn book smell, and not necessarily singing all the words in the book, rather my own words about my puppy in my pocket collection, which was the intense interest of the moment.

At the age 6 was the first time that I remember being upset within church. I was in Sunday School with other children I had grown up with. It was in a small room with wooden flooring, yellow walls and the tables that can be collapsed and stored. There were about five other children in the room with two adults. I was wearing a dress and the rather large round 90s-style glasses with a pink and white mottled frame. I saw one of the other children do something—I cannot remember quite what—and I did this too. The older of the two adults screaming at me. Being on the receiving end of what felt in my body as screaming resulted in a strong feeling of shame. Why had I got screamed at and not the other child? I did not know what I had done was wrong, or not allowed. The shame flushes through me in strong waves and immobilizes me. I burst into tears. I could not keep it all in. I cried and cried, my eyes red and sore and looking even redder with my pink and white mottled lenses and my bright auburn hair. "I hate her," I thought. The rest of what happened next is a haze, but every time I saw this woman afterwards I felt a distinct lack of trust and unease. "You're not nice." "I can't trust you won't burst into a screaming rage at me again." It was not only the thoughts I experienced, but a feeling came over me of shame of wrongdoing (even though I did not know what I had done wrong). I put my guard up—I did not want to be in a similar situation again. I kept a watch out for what could be deemed as "right" and "good," and censored myself in light of this. I had to protect myself from this sort of outburst from happening again.

I continued to protect myself. As I reached the end of primary school, I felt increasingly 'not a part' of the core group of children I had grown up with. I was different, but I did not know why. Sunday school was loud and busy, and without a peer for me to hide behind, I felt ever more exposed. I felt awkward and out of place, and not quite at ease with the adults in the room not because they were bad, but because I questioned how to interact. I did not know what to say or how to be a part of conversations. This came to a head one Sunday, when I would not go into Sunday School. Having left the pew, I was unable to enter the hall Sunday school was in. It was in an extension to the main church, and you left the conversation area to your left and passed the big open space, and went down a flight of very 1970s looking stairs with a metal handrail and a red plastic covering on this handrail. I froze and cried, I could not physically go in. I was overwhelmed with anxiety, my body would not let me walk into the hall where they met. It was loud. It was busy. It was an assault on my senses. Seeing that I was frozen, one of my parents suggested we went to the McDonalds round the corner as a space to go and calm down in. McDonalds was not far from the church, it was along the road and a right turn. I do not remember much from the walk, but I do remember being sat in McDonalds and how bright the sunshine was that day. It was bursting through the front—where I was sat on the high tables and stools that I enjoyed sitting at. I remember the relief from pressures and demands, the freedom to "be me." I also remember a bit of shame that I felt in relation to the fact I had pulled one of my parents out of church—somewhere they enjoyed and felt liked they belonged—to sit in McDonalds with me in a place of safety, away from the jumble of the Sunday School hall.

I did not cope with starting secondary school and became increasingly aware that something was different about me. I struggled to make deep friendships and to be seen as anything other than "quiet and smart." I did not know how to navigate the social world, which was becoming more and more complicated. I was also withdrawing from more and more, including from Sunday School which I stopped attending regularly. I received my second diagnosis of autism in the midst of this turmoil. Two young people (one who I had known through church for years but not really spoken to, one who I went to primary school with and knew through a children's club) tried to persuade me to go. I felt like I was being pushed into going. I was so scared of physically getting up and going and sitting in a room full of teenagers who I felt "outsiders" from. I did not feel comfortable at being in such a space as my anxiety was so high, I wanted to stay safe with my parents. The new assistant minister's wife was another person who tried to encourage me. I still felt out of place when I went. I saw cliques and groups like little fences of young people, with no gate to let me in. I controlled what others saw when I did make it in—I felt unable to take part in the discussions in Sunday School for fear of saying something that would expose me as even more different.

Analytical considerations

Even before I knew I was different, I was managing the impressions others had of me to be more palatable and acceptable. I felt marked as an outsider (Becker, 2008). Occasions where the environment was too much for me, for example the hustle and bustle of Sunday School with the sensory assault of complex noise and light, I felt I had to not show the overwhelm and distress I felt. The sensory experiences I had were in line with those of other neurodivergent people, in particular Autistic people, who experience sensory differences (O'Neill & Jones, 1997). I did this through either removing myself from the situation, so as not to discredit myself (Goffman, 1963), or through passing by copying other children to play down discreditable aspects of my identity (Goffman, 1963) to expose me as "deviant." During these critical incidents in my story, one commonality across them all is how I managed others' impressions of me (Goffman, 1959). Even though I did not know I was Autistic, I did recognize how I needed to be acutely aware that how I appeared to others in social contexts impacted what attitudes were held of me. I knew that if I let the mask "slip," that there would be repercussions. This fear of being exposed encapsulates Scambler's (2004) felt stigma; I was fearful of being exposed as "lesser," which is in keeping with Goffman's (1963) definition of what a stigma is.

On the occasions I did not meet others' expectations, such as the time in Sunday School where I was told off, I felt exposed as "deviant." In that moment, I had moved from being a person without a stigma to someone who was not meeting standards and expectations set for me (Misztal, 2001). Whereas some children could have shaken this off, this felt like a dagger to my heart, and that my veneered impression of being a "good girl" had broken. Although this did not expose me as Autistic, it did expose me as "maskless." My reaction to be being "caught out" is of particular analytical interest. I had been exposed as unable to deal with the unexpected, raised voices and being "wrong." I now acted with suspicion and with a guard up, disrupting the bidirectional and intersubjective bond of belonging within that one context.

Felt stigma and the fear of being exposed could be said to drive the passing I did within Church contexts. Employing impression management to increase my acceptability and gain a sense of perceived belonging complicates some theological stances, whereby belonging and welcome are center piece to Church. Perhaps this is indicative of the values and attitudes churchgoers may bring into a Church context (Webb-Mitchell, 1994, p. 79), which have been found previously to influence attitudes toward autism in church contexts (Waldock & Forrester-Jones, 2020). Furthermore, the use of impression management to maximize inclusion and feelings of belonging further demonstrates the socially situated nature of feelings of belonging for many individuals, and echoes belonging as intersubjective (Mahar et al., 2013). Through feeling I did not fit the norms within the church, both with ideas that were biblically based and "secular" attitudes, I felt belonging was contingent on meeting the norms of the church and presenting myself as a person without a stigma.

When I did know and accepted that I was neurodivergent

That moment I knew. I had recently left a job where I was trying to be someone who I was not. I had spent years at this point, trying to present a version of myself that was palatable for others to try to fit in. Often results worked in the short term, but the impact on me meant I could not keep it up in the long term. Parts of me would leak out and others would pick up on this, leading to me leaving places including workplaces and friendship groups. I could not keep forcing myself into situations that were making me sick and overwhelmed, and where I felt broken. It was a true penny-drop moment being stood in my bedroom opposite the wheely stacker next to my bed. "I am not just anxious, I have not only got social anxiety; I am Autistic." It was at that moment I started to own being Autistic. I had to stop forcing myself to be someone who I am not. I did not know as much as I do now, I did not know that much. But it was at that moment some of my boundaries were redrawn and a new understanding of myself began. I started exploring through Facebook about autism and Autistic people, and found a whole new language to express what I was experiencing.

I started being more vocal about my needs, I remember writing on a Facebook post something about being Autistic and finding the noise in church difficult. By now we were attending Church B. One member of church leadership wanted to know more, and we started discussions about accessibility in the foyer of Church B. We were sitting in the corner on those typical church chairs—pine wood with red cushions. The light in the room was bright. I felt seen. I felt validated. We met and planned actions and she took my experiences seriously. I remember leaving the conversations we had feeling full of energy and hope. I uncovered some of the layers of hiding I had built over the years, which felt exposed and uncomfortable.

One frustration I did experience was lack of interest from others in church leadership. I felt like a portcullis had been dropped: not here, not us. I continued to talk and share, I continued to ask how we can do things differently. When I got my hands dirty, such as helping with the tech desk, I felt as if the responsibility to make everything more accessible landed on my shoulders. I was sitting in the corner of the church behind this tech desk—which could be seen as a powerful spot—but felt unable to advocate for the changes needed. I was scared. Even though I had started to "out" myself, I still was lacking the words and confidence to say what I needed and the more I outed myself and stated my needs, the more out of place I felt. When I said I was in pain with the volume and complexity of the noise, I remained unheard. Silence. When church leadership changed, I felt even more unheard. I ended up sitting inside the main church very uncomfortable, in pain and overwhelmed, suppressing my autistic overwhelm and distress with a carefully constructed "mask" of nothingness. Or I sat outside and felt physically excluded and unable to join in, signaling my "autistic-ness" with headphones and being sat apart.

It was also a similar time that I spoke to church leadership about how excluded I felt within the church, and the difficulties and distress I was feeling. I went to speak to them one afternoon—thinking perhaps we can move forward. This meeting was in a side room of the church: However I was faced with this statement: "it's a journey." A journey to make a space that works for everyone, and time to consider. I walked away feeling unease, which then turned into anger. "How could they dismiss my feelings?" "Why could they not see the problem?" They had not taken how I experience the world seriously and emphasized the need for patience on my part. This felt like my distress was seen as a slight inconvenience. Because my access needs were not visible to the obvious eye, they were played down in that moment. I saw them as not real enough, and not real enough of pain to qualify for something to be done.

Analytical considerations

When I did have positive interactions, I started to feel the strongest sense of belonging I had ever experienced within a church congregation. I was not managing the impressions I left on others as much and being accepted for who I was, rather than what was expected of me. Individuals were proactive in listening to me and taking me seriously, rather than discrediting my words due to my "stigmatized identity." I was valued for how wonderfully made I am whilst also respecting that I did not wish to be a "self-narrating zoo exhibit."

However after a change in leadership, my "stigmatized identity" caused further issues, and I became the "impossible subject" (as described by Abraham, 2009). I was marked out as different. I felt "discredited," because I wore headphones and sat apart from others in church. I did not meet the norms set by the church. I could not manage the complexity and volume of the sound, physically setting me apart through the visual cues I wore (headphones) and the places I sat (outside). I was reminded I needed to conform to belong, echoed in Rafferty's (2022, p. 118) analysis of Spies' (2021) experience within churches. In these cases, I experienced enacted stigma (Scambler, 2004) rather than felt stigma. I was excluded by the clash of my own needs with the desires of church leadership. I was a "problem to be managed" (Raffety, 2022, p. 23). Church leadership knew about the support needs I had; I was not fearful of being 'outed' as Autistic or others finding out I about me. . I did not meet the norms of being able to worship in such a space, or at least not without physically removing myself and not advocating for my needs. The anger and the frustration I experienced at the denial of action was epistemic injustice (Fricker, 2007). Silencing in this manner, though stating "it's a journey" and placation minimized my distress, and further excluded me. Cults of "normalcy" (as theorized by Davis, 1995 and van Ommen & Endress, 2022) shaped how church was "done," including how we worship and what we subject our bodies to in church. Normalcy excluded me, and I was an outsider. For those who did not know me in the church, nor really understood the way I experienced the world, I continued to experience felt stigma (Scambler, 2004). Although I was "out," not everyone in the church knew each other, nor understood neurodivergent lived experience. Through experiencing both felt and enacted stigma, along with the lack of meeting norms through passing and other impression strategies, I felt increasingly as if I did belong. Acceptance appeared contingent on meeting the norms of the church and being able to compartmentalize and suppress overwhelm, whilst passing as a person without a stigma. Through asking questions of the leadership team regarding access requirements and needs, I was placed in the position of "impossible subject." Neurodivergent people as impossible subjects can also be seen in the stories Raffety (2022, p. 65) collects in her ethnography, where Autistic people's needs are seen as "too difficult" or "untenable" by church leadership or volunteers. I understood that through disclosure and advocacy, challenging how the way church was "done" excluded me; perhaps through a lack of provision, but ultimately through me not being heard or listened to.

Conclusion

Belonging for neurodivergent people in congregations, and how neurodivergent people are perceived and interact in majority neuro-normative cultures, are important focal points for discussion when considering welcome or inclusion. In relation to my research question, being neurodivergent did appear to impact how I experienced belonging within congregational settings. Firstly through impression management prior to me realizing my neurodivergent identity, and then after I "came out," being perceived as discredited due to being neurodivergent. Both these experiences complicated my experience of belonging within congregational settings, echoing findings from Jacobs and Richardson (2022). As my Autistic identity became more and more central to how I understood and processed the world, I found myself challenging whether I should pass to fit in, and outing myself as "discredited." Neurodivergent bodies and brains mediate how we belong through challenging norms and others' standards, leading to some of us becoming "impossible subjects." Neurodivergent people as 'impossible subjects' sits in opposition to all, including neurodivergent people, being made in God's image (van Ommen, 2022a).

Managing stigma in order to feel a sense of belonging also sits in conflict with theological underpinnings of the importance of belonging within Christianity and churches. It places churches as socially situated contexts with influence from the secular world (Webb-Mitchell, 1994, p. 79). Furthermore, it poses questions on the level of theological interrogation belonging for marginalized groups has received to date. This conflict also highlights the theological obligation to take Autistic, and other neurodivergent experiences seriously (van Ommen, 2022a) and how this aligns with how we "do church." Excluding people intentionally or inadvertently from worship services is problematic (van Ommen 2022b; Waldock, 2022), therefore highlighting the urgent need for churches to consider how we 'do church', and how much 'cults of normalcy' (see van Ommen & Endress, 2022) are operationalized within churches. Expectations of neurodivergent people need to move away from meeting majority-set norms in order to belong, as argued also by van Ommen (2022a), and should move away from meeting these norms. Acceptance should be intersubjective and not merely based on those with a stigma meeting the norms of those who do not have a stigma (van Ommen, 2022a; Waldock & Forrester-Jones, 2020).

In terms of how this autoethnographic account further complicates biblical understandings of belonging, it challenges leaders and congregants to consider how power dynamics and perceptions shape experiences of belonging. It poses the question of how we should frame belonging, and if normative belonging should in fact be a goal in theological discourse, sociological and theological research, and practice. Perhaps a better goal is the facilitation of spaces where neurodiverse relationships can thrive, and power relationships are examined.

Notes

1. Goffman (1963) refers to individuals without a stigma as "normals". Given the main tenet of the neurodiversity paradigm is the inherent value of all brains and cognition (Walker, 2021), and how "normal" can be value laden to mean neurotypical by some scientists and researchers within autism studies, "individuals without a stigma" or "individuals who are not stigmatised" will be used in lieu.
2. Discreditable identity: an identity that is socially devalued and concealable from, or made invisible to others
3. Sociologists may argue that they are less interested in stigma when the stigmatised individual is not aware of it (Goffman, 1963, p. 93). However in relation to my story, I would argue I was always stigmatised – not necessarily as Autistic – but as "weird", "odd", "shy" or "strange". I would therefore posit that in the case of people who are neurodivergent from birth, the stories pre-identification remain relevant to social stigma theory.

Acknowledgments

The author would like to thank the following individuals for helping show the "clutter and dust" of the narrative, and proofreading: Dr Naomi Lawson Jacobs, Fiona MacMillan, Holly Smith, Katrine Callendar.

Disclosure statement

No potential conflict of interest was reported by the author(s).

ORCID

Krysia Emily Waldock ⓘ http://orcid.org/0000-0001-9631-3930

References

Abraham, I. (2009). 'Out to get us': Queer Muslims and the clash of sexual civilisations in Australia. *Contemporary Islam, 3*(1), 79–97. https://doi.org/10.1007/s11562-008-0078-3

Anderson, C. L. (2020). Recovery from relinquishment: Forgiving my birth mother. My journey from 1954 to today. *The Qualitative Report, 25*(11), 3794–3809.

Becker, H. S. (2008). *Outsiders.* Simon and Schuster.

Bochner, A. P., & Ellis, C. (2016). *Evocative autoethnography: Writing lives and telling stories.* Routledge.

Bochner, A. P. (2017). Heart of the matter: A mini-manifesto for autoethnography. *International Review of Qualitative Research, 10*(1), 67–80. https://doi.org/10.1525/irqr.2017.10.1.67

Carter, E. W., Biggs, E. E., & Boehm, T. L. (2016). Being present versus having a presence: Dimensions of belonging for young people with disabilities and their families. *Christian Education Journal: Research on Educational Ministry, 13*(1), 127–146. https://doi.org/10.1177/073989131601300109

Chang, H. (2008). *Autoethnography as method.* Routledge.

Cooper, R., & Lilyea, B. (2022). I'm Interested in Autoethnography, but How Do I Do It? *The Qualitative Report, 27*(1), 197–208. https://doi.org/10.46743/2160-3715/2022.5288

Davis, L. (1995). *Enforcing normalcy: Disability, deafness, and the body.* Verso.

Edwards, J. (2021). Ethical autoethnography: Is it possible? *International Journal of Qualitative Methods, 20*, 160940692199530. https://doi.org/10.1177/1609406921995306

Eiesland, N. L. (1994). *The disabled God: Toward a liberatory theology of disability.* Abingdon Press.

Ellis, C. (2007). Telling secrets, revealing lives: Relational ethics in research with intimate others. *Qualitative Inquiry, 13*(1), 3–29. https://doi.org/10.1177/1077800406294947

Ellis, C., Adams, T. E., & Bochner, A. P. (2011). Autoethnography: An overview. *Historical social research/Historische sozialforschung, 12*(1), 273–290.

Etherington, K. (2007). Ethical research in reflexive relationships. *Qualitative Inquiry, 13*(5), 599–616. https://doi.org/10.1177/1077800407301175

Fricker, M. (2007). *Epistemic injustice: Power and the ethics of knowing.* Oxford University Press.

Frith, U. (2003). *Autism: Explaining the enigma.* Blackwell Publishing.

Goffman, E. (1959). *The presentation of self in everyday life.* Penguin.

Goffman, E. (1963). *Stigma: Notes on the management of spoiled identity.* Penguin.

Gutiérrez, G. (1973). *A theology of liberation.* 1st (Spanish) ed. Lima, Peru, 1971; 1st English ed Orbis Books.

Holman Jones, S. (2016). Living bodies of thought: The "critical" in critical autoethnography. *Qualitative Inquiry, 22*(4), 228–237. https://doi.org/10.1177/1077800415622509

Jacobs, N. L. (2022). A story like mine. *Canadian Journal of Theology, Mental Health and Disability, 2*(2), 132–142.

Jacobs, N., & Richardson, E. (2022). *At the gates – disability, justice and the churches.* Darton, Longman & Todd.

Javaid, A. (2020). The haunting of shame: Autoethnography and the multivalent stigma of being queer, Muslim, and single. *Symbolic Interaction, 43*(1), 72–101. https://doi.org/10.1002/symb.441

Kramer, H., & Sprenger, J. (1928/1971 [1489]). *Malleus Maleficarum.* (M. Summers, Trans.). Arrow Books.

Leary, M. R. (2010). Affiliation, acceptance, and belonging: The pursuit of interpersonal connection. In S. T. Fiske, D. T. Gilbert, & G. Lindzey (Eds.), *Handbook of social psychology* (pp. 864–897). John Wiley & Sons, Inc.

Mahar, A. L., Cobigo, V., & Stuart, H. (2013). Conceptualizing belonging. *Disability and Rehabilitation, 35*(12), 1026–1032. https://doi.org/10.3109/09638288.2012.717584

Memmott, A. (2019). Belonging – about autism and church. *Ann's Autism Blog.* http://annsautism.blogspot.com/2020/09/belonging-about-autism-and-church.html

Miles, M. (2001). Martin Luther and childhood disability in 16th century Germany: What did he write? What did he say? *Journal of Religion, Disability & Health, 5*(4), 5–36. doi: 10.1300/J095v05n04_02

Miller, D., Rees, J., & Pearson, A. (2021). "Masking is life": Experiences of masking in autistic and nonautistic adults. *Autism in Adulthood : Challenges and Management, 3*(4), 330–338. https://doi.org/10.1089/aut.2020.0083

Misztal, B. A. (2001). Normality and trust in Goffman's theory of interaction order. *Sociological Theory, 19*(3), 312–324. https://doi.org/10.1111/0735-2751.00143

Moltmann, J. (1998). Liberate yourselves by accepting one another. In N. L. Eiesland & D. E. Saliers (Eds.), *Human disability and the service of God: Reassessing religious practice* (pp. 105–122). Abingdon Press.

O'Neill, M., & Jones, R. S. (1997). Sensory-perceptual abnormalities in autism: A case for more research? *Journal of Autism and Developmental Disorders, 27*(3), 283–293. https://doi.org/10.1023/a:1025850431170

Pardede, S., Gausel, N., & Høie, M. M. (2020). Revisiting the "the breakfast club": Testing different theoretical models of belongingness and acceptance (and social self-representation). *Frontiers in Psychology, 11*, 604090. https://doi.org/10.3389/fpsyg.2020.604090

Rambo, C. (2016). Strange accounts: Applying for the department chair position and writing threats and secrets "in play". *Journal of Contemporary Ethnography, 45*(1), 3–33. https://doi.org/10.1177/0891241615611729

Radulski, E. M. (2022). Conceptualising autistic masking, camouflaging, and neurotypical privilege: Towards a minority group model of neurodiversity. *Human Development, 66*(2), 113–127. https://doi.org/10.1159/000524122

Raffery, E. (2022). *From inclusion to justice: Disability, ministry and congregational leadership.* Baylor University Press.

Scambler, G. (2004). Re-framing stigma: Felt and enacted stigma and challenges to the sociology of chronic and disabling conditions. *Social Theory & Health, 2*(1), 29–46. https://doi.org/10.1057/palgrave.sth.8700012

Scambler, G. (2009). Health-related stigma. *Sociology of Health & Illness, 31*(3), 441–455. https://doi.org/10.1111/j.1467-9566.2009.01161.x

Sedgewick, F., Hull, L., & Ellis, H. (2021). *Autism and masking: How and why people do it, and the impact it can have.* Jessica Kingsley Publishers.

Spies, M. (2021). from belonging as supercrip to misfitting as crip: Journeying through seminary. *Journal of Disability & Religion*, *25*(3), 296–311. https://doi.org/10.1080/233 12521.2021.1895028

Van Ommen, A. L. (2022a). Re-imagining church through autism: A Singaporean case study. *Practical Theology*, *15*(6), 508–519. https://doi.org/10.1080/1756073X.2022.2080630

Van Ommen, A. L. (2022b). When community gets in the way: Reflections on autism and worship. *Reformed World*, *70*(1), 48–55.

van Ommen, A. L., & Endress, T. (2022). Reframing liturgical theology through the lens of autism: A qualitative study of autistic experiences of worship. *Studia Liturgica*, *52*(2), 219–234. https://doi.org/10.1177/00393207221111573

Waldock, K. E., & Forrester-Jones, R. (2020). An exploratory study of attitudes toward autism amongst church-going Christians in the South East of England, United Kingdom. *Journal of Disability & Religion*, *24*(4), 349–370. https://doi.org/10.1080/23312521.2020.1776667

Waldock, K. (2021). "Doing church" during COVID-19: An autistic reflection on online church. *Canadian Journal of Theology, Mental Health and Disability*, *1*(1), 66–70.

Waldock, K. (2022). Inclusive Online Church Consultation: What did we find out? *Inclusive Church*. https://www.inclusive-church.org/2022/01/18/inclusive-online-church-consultation-what-did-we-find-out/

Waldock, K. E., McCarthy, M., & Bradshaw, J. (2021). Conceptualising belonging: The views of Autistic people (poster 2021). Kent Graduate Researcher Showcase. https://doi.org/10.13140/RG.2.2.10271.69280

Waldock, K. E., & Sango, P. N. (2023). Autism, faith and Churches: Where we have been and where we go next. *Theology in Scotland*, *30*(1), 47–57. https://doi.org/10.15664/tis.v30i1.2578

Walker, N. (2021). *Neuroqueer Heresies. Notes on the neurodiversity paradigm, autistic empowerment, and postnormal possibilities*. Autonomous Press.

Waltz, M. (2013). *Autism: A social and medical history*. Palgrave Macmillan.

Webb-Mitchell, B. (1994). *Unexpected guests at God's banquet: Welcoming people with disabilities into the church*. The Crossroad Publishing Company.

Peculiar Theological Education

Claire Williams

ABSTRACT

Theological education has yet to grapple with the complexities of autistic lives and the wider neurodiversity movement. This article discusses the ways in which theological education is complicit in the epistemic oppression of autistic students and lecturers. It proposes that autistic theology can be called "peculiar" and that so also can theological education be made peculiar for autistic theology students. A pedagogy for autistic theological education is proposed *via* engagement with Paulo Freire, black and feminist theologies. Such a theology, in a confessional Christian context is described as post-Pentecostal conscientization and seeks a community of students and scholars that treat the classroom as holy ground for autistic lives.

Introduction

Autism is contentiously defined. There are differences in belief about the causes and origins of autism and the nature by which is should be described (Dinishak & Akhtar, 2023). This results in opposing views of whether autism is a "condition" that should be treated medically or a consequence of natural human diversity. If the prevailing medical opinion is adhered to then autism is a disability, possibly with biological origins, that has poor outcomes and it will negatively affect the flourishing of the individual (as described in Chapman & Carel, 2022, pp. 615–616). It is considered a nonstandard way of human life that should be considered a deficit. The neurodiversity paradigm describes autism and latterly other differences in brains (e.g. ADHD, bipolar, dyslexia) not as a medical problem but as an aspect of human variance that is not well accommodated by society (Dinishak & Akhtar, 2023). Damian Milton, for example, has suggested that autism could be constructed as a difference in mutual cognition between the autistic person and the neurotypical person (Milton, 2012). Neurodiversity models of autism reject understandings of autism as a lack and hold to account society for affecting disabling conditions upon autistic people who then fail to thrive. The neurodiversity paradigm is therefore political as well as social, noting power differences and situations of inequality as primary issues of discrimination. This is in comparison to medical models which understand the impairment of autism as the cause of suffering in the autistic individual (Chapman & Carel, 2022). This paper follows the neurodiversity paradigm as the primary narrative and descriptive tool by which autism can be understood. "Autism is highly heterogeneous and is experienced differently by different individuals and within the same individual across their life span and across contexts" (Dinishak & Akhtar, 2023, p. 4). This means that any quest for integration and understanding of autism requires individual understandings rather than generalizations and for recognition that descriptions, particularly medical, fail to serve the variance and diversity of human life.

An understanding of how autistic people experience theological education and are best served by it is lacking from both scholarly and popular literature. Provisional and seminal studies in the field of autism and theology are suggestive of a need to understand how autism is both served and failed by the church but this has yet to engage with the formal work of theological education (Macaskill, 2021; Rapley, 2021). These works imply a distinct autistic approach to theology, worship and relationships with God (Van Ommen & Endress, 2022). Indeed, Stuart Rapley indicates that autistic individuals have distinct conceptions of God, interactions with the Bible and experiences of prayer (Rapley, 2021, pp. 51, 72 & 89).

These differences articulated in the studies about cognition and in the ethnographic work of theologians can be said to represent an epistemic difference relating to the gaining and sharing of knowledge or knowledge production. Miranda Fricker describes instances of "conveying knowledge to others by telling them, and making sense of our social experiences" as "everyday epistemic practices" (Fricker, 2011, p. 1). Yet epistemic injustice is served when these differences are neither articulated nor examined and when those who are different in their knowing—both of God and of theology—are marginalized and discredited. For Fricker such injustice is to do with the receipt of the testimony of the knower and this is defined as "*identity-prejudicial credibility deficit*" (Fricker, 2011, p. 28). For autistic people whose experience is received as flawed or unworthy they are subject to such injustice. In keeping with the emphases of the neurodiversity movement and the questioning of medical models I will describe autism as subject to injustice and prejudice. This injustice stems from the normalization of neurotypical lived experiences and the rejection of differences in cognition both within and without the church.

In this article I consider theological education that is confessional, found most commonly in seminaries and institutions that train lay and ordained ministers. By this I refer to education that is founded upon a confession of faith and is described as formational in a given faith context. I am not considering theological education in the secular university, which requires a different flavor of analysis. I choose confessional theological education because that is my own experience and I am therefore aided in the reflexive task of theology by speaking of and to what I am situated in. I also find that there is much constructive scholarship that can be said in this field bridging as it does academic and spiritual formation.

Peculiarity

Autistic theology within the neurodiversity paradigm should be disruptive. In the same manner that liberation theologies have sought to challenge establish norms and describe that which has not been given voice before, so also should theologies that are self-identified as autistic. Part of this task is to reclaim the pejorative and negative language of medicalised autism studies and transform it for use in the defence and reclamation of autism theologies for autistic people. To this end, I write, as I have done before, of the peculiarity of autism (Williams, 2023). Autistic theology is peculiar because it disrupts social expectations. Autistic people are described as being socially uncoordinated, unable to reach other people and failures at the requirements of relationships that make them "normal" (Biklen & Attfield, 2005). However, this normativity is prescribed by neurotypical people in neurotypical ways that are deterministic of the failure of autistic people to reach such expectations. Although this is challenged by autistic scholars in theology it continues to pervade in the church, particularly in the theology that informs it as will be shown below but also in the varying experiences of the church and knowledge and understanding in church congregations about autism (Waldock & Forrester-Jones, 2020).[1]

The neurodiversity paradigm seeks to broaden our understanding of autism and other and to engage awareness of the diversity and plurality of human existence and cognition. In a journal edition such as this further explanation of the aim of the neurodiversity paradigm is unnecessary. Where it intersects with my argument is that neurodiversity speaks against the epistemic assumptions of normativity. "Peculiar" theological education does not work against this claim but toward the same goals. Calling autistic theology and autistic theological education "peculiar" endeavors to reclaim dehumanizing language. Autistic people have long been considered odd, strange, and weird (Limburg, 2021). In the same way as some theorists reclaim "crip" for their examinations of disability so also can autistic theology lay hands on the derogatory language that has oppressed them and subversively claim it as their own. This is my rational for describing autistic theological education as "peculiar." It is peculiar because it is specific—it represents a group of people who travel through the world in a different register. It is peculiar because it is located and historical—it speaks for those whose lived experiences which are unrecognized and not described. In the manner of liberation theologies it recognizes the need for theological voice into specific experiences and sites of oppression. It is peculiar because it recognizes diversity and embraces it.

Christian theological education

Eve Parker's timely and troubling work "Trust in Theological Education" is a useful theological partner for an autistic theology of confessional higher education. In her work she questions the trustworthiness of theological education for anyone who is not white, male, middle-class and heteronormative (Parker, 2022, p. 1). Theological education, she claims, has been "complicit in validating systems of injustices and perpetuating the conditions of coloniality, inequality and dominion." (Parker, 2022, p. 164). It cannot be trusted because only certain voices can be heard. Trust is closely correlated with credibility. In the language of Miranda Fricker, credibility is the authenticity given to a speaker by those that hear them (Fricker, 2011, pp. 16–17). Both trust and credibility are foundational to higher education. To whom is credibility given? What sort of knowledge is worth learning? What reproduction of this knowledge is sufficient for passing grades and acceptability? Parker describes the regulation of such knowledge. Those who are in power are those that decide upon the suitability of knowledge and that which is sufficient, is credible for theological studies. The task of the educator is to take this approved knowledge and transfer it to the student. Following Paulo Freire, Parker highlights the subject of this knowledge power dynamic is the "ignorant" empty vessel. The "meek" student must accept their knowledge and in so doing perform their role in the cycle of education (Freire, 2017, p. 45).

The theology of the church has often failed in its task to bring good news to all people, it has instead perpetrated prejudice and dehumanization,

> Systems of hate that have sought to shame certain bodies and inflict violence on bodies with their ideologies of oppression – ideologies that want to kill black bodies, convert queer bodies, slut-shame women's bodies, deprive poor bodies, silence colonialized bodies, degrade so-called 'disabled bodies', mock working class bodies and subjugate Dalit bodies. (Parker, 2022, p. 30)

To this I would add, the shame of an autistic bodymind. Autistic shame of damaged friendships, failure to engage in churches, othering by society and invalidation of choices and ways of being cause great pain and suffering for the autistic person (Williams, 2022, p. 196). Autistic people are prone to feel shame and be traumatized (Gates, 2019). I have written elsewhere that this is also the case in the church where prevailing ideas of normativity and of disability create a culture of "not good enough" and incompleteness and where unmet needs cause long term invalidation (Williams, 2022). Freire's twofold task of liberating pedagogies first requires the oppressed to critically recognize their situation, to engage in conscientization (Freire, 2017, p. 21). Conscientization is the ability to understand the world and the levels of consciousness of reality (Bridges Johns, 2010, p. 30). To achieve this critical distance to truly describe the world as experienced by the person who is oppressed is the process of "critical transitivity" which is achieved "when humans become subjects and engage themselves in shaping reality through cultural action" (Bridges Johns, 2010, p. 32).

For autistic people this requires understanding their place on Parker's list above. They too are oppressed by Christian theology and those that use it to shape individuals into images of itself. For if autistic people are metaphors for failure to know and understand God (McFall, 2022) or used in philosophical theology as foils to full humanity (Stump, 2010, p. 68) then it is challenging to imagine a situation in which theological education allows for the full human flourishing of autistic students. This is a form of epistemic injustice.

Cornwall et al. (2022) write that our self-understanding is part of our own epistemic authority. We give value, they say following Talia Mae Bettcher, to the stories based on first-person's experience. It is unlikely, we usually think, that someone will be wrong about themselves. They write of trans people and those with intersex characteristics and claim that the stories and narratives written *about* these groups that are "others" assessments of what these person's bodies mean and signify are privileged above their own' (Cornwall et al., 2022). These are theological accounts of trans and intersex bodies that do not account for the first-person experience. This they say is a "testimonial injustice" such as the type described by Miranda Fricker. It is apparent that a similar testimonial injustice is served to autistic people in theology. They have not had the ability to describe their own experience or their own bodies but are subject to descriptions *about* them. Such descriptions, as already noted, are damaging accounts of failures to reach the divine because of "selfishness" or being used as metaphors for sub humanity. Autistic testimony of lived lives in the presence of God, in the Christian community are relegated to untruth and are denied epistemic credibility.

Anthony Reddie describes liberative theological education for black theology as one which critically reflects upon the nature of the oppressed existence (Reddie, 2023, p. 198). This includes recognition that the authoritative, "white" teaching of Euro-American theology that is considered "correct" does not have enough of a relationship with anti-racist and ethical behavior (Reddie, 2023, p. 199). To cast this notion of critical relationship with "correct" theological education with its relationship to prejudicial autistic behavior is fruitful. In keeping with the critical questions that Parker raises, an autistic theological education should trouble normative descriptions of humanity that exclude the autistic person and do not enable their flourishing nor their contribution. This includes the need to recognize that theology does not advocate for freedom of oppression for autistic people. Grant Macaskill cites examples of autism described as demon possession, that it is a problem in need of if not a cure then divine healing, of hermeneutical methods that do not allow for a picture of autism that is sufficient or life giving (Macaskill, 2022). This compounds the narrative that is propagated in medical models that autism is a deviation from the norm, a problem in need of a solution. With the authority of biblical interpretation and the testimonial power of scholarly voices the theological message is profoundly damaging when autistic people are considered also to be spiritually other, questionably positioned in God's world, of dubiously and troubling origins that have only negative theological explanations.

Valorizing of neurotypical rationality in higher education and in Christian theology deprioritises those who engage with the world in cognitively different ways. Parker notes that knowledge begins in bodies, the way in which bodies are subject to the world around them informs their knowing. For Parker "pedagogies of whiteness" silence bodies that tell different stories. The knowledge of particular bodies that are not white, male, middle-class and heteronormative are silenced and their experiences are "reduced to anecdotes" (Parker, 2022, p. 31). Thus their body's experience is disowned by themselves as subjects in an education system that does not recognize their bodily knowledge. What does this look like for autistic bodyminds? Recent debates about the prevalence of autism suggest anything between 1 in 100 people and 1 in 50 (Macaskill, 2021, p. 1). There is little awareness of autistic lives and representation in theology and theological education and the choices of the leaders of theological seminaries and curricula. Autistic stories are not told in theology and therefore not represented in theological education. Their experience is not heard, not mentioned nor recognized. The stories of autism are tragedies in search of cures, of parental fragmentation in light of diagnoses, of problems without solutions, or othering and isolation, they are also embodied stories, of sensory sensitivities—finding church too loud or too quiet, of stimming—both wanted and unwanted, of language—its absence and its unwelcome abundance (Williams, 2023, pp. 107–139). These disruptive autistic bodies have no recorded place in the rationality of Christian theology, as we see if the examples from theology above. They are used to illustrate unwelcome ideas rather than the love of God and the fellowship of the church.

What can Christian theological education be?

It is known that autistic people learn differently and are affected by classroom and seminar room environments in ways that are different to neurotypical students. They are also likely to have more trouble adapting to transitions to higher education and be undiagnosed and therefore at increased risk of adverse consequences for wellbeing (Pinder-Amaker, 2014). Theological education for autistic people should have a liberative strand, incorporating Freire's task of liberating all who are subject to oppression and also all whom are the oppressors. It is not sufficient, says Freire, to simply switch places with the oppressors having internalized the oppressor's image and made it our own (Freire, 2017, p. 21). For autistic thinking this might appear as prioritizing autistic rationalities at the expense of neurotypical rationalities which would then do that which Freire warns against, switching the valued knowledge around—valuing autistic knowledge and prejudicing neurotypical knowledge. Rather, all forms of theological knowledge should be welcome.

Classroom – presiding together in the Spirit

Rather, an autistic theological pedagogy requires a description of the mutuality that is found in the Christian community that is one in the Spirit of God. This Christological and penumatological anthropology locates *all* who participate in the work of theological education. For the autistic student or the autistic teacher they are humanized in this process, not because before this they were not human, but because of their situation of oppression which dehumanized them. The theological classroom, as I shall show, becomes a site of conscientization.

Both student and teacher have roles in the liberative autistic theological education. Cheryl Bridge Johns in her work on Paulo Freire in a Pentecostal context argues for humanization as a noteworthy concept of liberative theological education. She claims that whilst Freire seeks humanization in an earthly, historical sense the Pentecostal—and perhaps all Christians—can seek humanization pedagogically with an eschatological and soteriological lens (Bridge Johns, 2010, p. 122). Human dignity, even when denied in situations of oppression, is reflected in the divine gift of grace,

> Therefore, the church is to live as an alternative community, announcing God's gift of wholeness for the world and renouncing oppressive structures which do not see people as God sees them. (Bridge Johns, 2010, p. 122)

To do this the student of the theological academy can expect to be fully participant in the community that begins in the church and grows into confessional theological education.

Participating – the autistic student

Righting the wrongs of testimonial injustices is possible in the community of faith that facilitates theological learning and formation. Bridge Johns writes of the Pentecostal rites that facilitate conscientization. These are common to Pentecostal and charismatic churches and affect Pentecostal catechism but are theologically profitable more broadly, in particular the role she notes of *testimony*. Testimony is a common practice in Pentecostal and charismatic congregations. It affords individuals the opportunity to stand up and give voice to their own experience, they speak and tell their stories. These stories can be of the mundane and the extraordinary, they can be profound and divine or quiet and hopeful. They can be stories of suffering and oppression as well as of triumph and overcoming. Bridge Johns describes testimony as "the means of meshing the realities of life with the ongoing story of the faith community" (Bridge Johns, 2010, p. 126). It allows individuals to understand their own reality, to transform it by placing it within a wider story of the Christian tradition and it provides an avenue for a person to speak their story and be heard in its telling. This particular tradition in one expression of the church has powerful heuristic potential.

Autistic lives navigate communication in a neurotypical world. They may speak and be misunderstood, they may never speak at all, they may stammer and stutter or speak unreliably. They may repeat words that they have heard elsewhere—echolalia (Cohn et al., 2022). The relationship between autism and orality is therefore troubling, the ability to tell stories and account for their lives does not match neurotypical methods of linear, spoken and written, assessed and accepted narratives. Yet Pentecostalism and charismatic churches have deep oral roots of knowing (Bridge Johns, 2010, p. 123). Rather than contradict these knowings the oral Pentecostal tradition comprised of testimony, songs and stories, as Bridge Johns describes, allows for the location of divinely inspired personal accounts to play a role in the theologizing of the autistic person.

To make this case requires a diversion into another Pentecostal/charismatic notion—that of speaking in tongues. Tongues speech is known as "glossolalia" and comprises of ecstatic utterances or previously unknown words, typically used as a way of exalting God (Acts 2 and Acts 10.46). This diversity of language used in praise of God mirrors the Babylonian plurality of voice. Rather than understanding this diversity as a negative and corrective act of a vengeful God attempting to divert human hubris it is a merciful act of divine compassion. Those who attempted to homogenize humanity, making it fit the same mold—perhaps the mold that Jennings (2020) describes as "whiteness"—are guilty of the judgment at Babel. They seek to make all people, think, speak and act in the same way and to condemn those who don't. The occupants of Babel sought to "make a name for themselves" and by so doing control their own historical destiny. Macchia (2012) argues that they did so by resisting the dispersal out of the Garden of Eden and by expecting that speaking in one tongue, speaking the language of Babel offers both promise now and eschatological hope that humanity can order and control and manage its own destiny. Speaking in one homogenous tongue becomes idolatrous, "for if this one language reaches and lays claim to the absolute, there is never any room for another idiom." (Macchia, 2012, p. 41). No other way of speaking becomes permissible or acceptable.

The autistic way of communication—through speech, signing, writing, pointing, noises and grunts—is unacceptable speech in the world today which reaches for the pride of Babel and silences other forms of communication. Tongues speech, glossolalia, speaks another word—a more communicable and hopeful word in an academy that homogenizes speech.

> All of them were filled with the Holy Spirit and began to speak in other languages, as the Spirit gave them utterance. (Acts 2.4)

At Pentecost there is a speech reversal, one which allows many voices to be uttered. This becomes a celebration of plurality, a divine initiated and sanctioned acceptance of different ways of speaking. These different ways of speaking are, necessarily, different ways of knowing also, for speech cannot be separated from the cognitive processes that surround it. Pentecost and the gift of speaking in tongues are a theological demand for epistemological justice. The inability to speak one's own story of autistic life in theological education because of assumptions of ignorance, or because of metaphors of unacceptability in theological discourse becomes reversed in the Pentecostal narrative.[2]

This allows for what Amos Yong calls the "democratization" of knowledge (Yong, 2020, p. 105). Following the prevailing view in higher education of constructivist learning, that the student and the teacher are co-creators in the construction of understanding and knowledge, Yong argues that this mutual testifying is theologically based. Rather than accept such pedagogies because it is the mainstream opinion the theological academy should accept it because it is the post-Pentecost nature of learning,

> Our present interconnected era of online students already socially embedded in multiple time zones and missionally engaged in various ecclesial-cultural contexts invites retrieval of the early church's Pentecost experience that amplifies rather than silences the many voices coming from and going to the ends of the earth. (Yong, 2020, p. 110)

Where Yong sees a new era of online and networked students studying in context we can also add disabled and neurodivergent students studying in a more accessible way, engaging in education with their own context and needs in mind. The many voices of students in their own context—be they missionary students as Yong suggests—or non-speaking autistic students working from their homes - are heard in the post-Pentecost theological academy that receives voices that speak against homogeny. The voice of the autistic student in this classroom, either in person or *via* an online arrangement, is the disruptive voice testifying to their lived experience and consequently enriching the theological academy. Such testifying need not be the public words of a conversion story as is commonly imagined, rather testimony offers a place and a presence, an acknowledgement of individual lives without prior assumptions.

Presiding – the autistic teacher

Not only does the student right testimonial injustices by speaking with confidence and freedom in the post-Pentecostal environment, so also the teacher is a facilitator of the liberative autistic theological education. For the purposes of this paper such a teacher is also autistic, because theological educators can also be autistic educators, such as myself. Nicola Slee (2020) writes of the work of the teacher in theological education being an act similar to liturgical presidency. She writes as a feminist scholar bringing to light what women's experiences are when they have long been silenced and overlooked. In the same way that women have experienced the hiddenness she writes of, so also have autistic people. Indeed, the presidency and authority as "teachers of the faith" that she writes of for women is almost unheard of in autistic people's lives. For an autistic theological educator there is much overlap with the unheard and unknown agency of women in theological education. It is the role of the teacher as one who presides over their classroom, who "sits in front of an assembly," who takes a role of authority and accompanies learners on their educational journey (Slee, 2020, p. 172).

The metaphor of presiding aids theological pedagogy in its liberative endeavor. The teacher or lecturer enables the learning of others as they hold in the midst of the classroom the potential of all the people in the room. There is, says Slee, a "kenotic quality to all teaching," where the teacher is, in the same way as a priest, self-emptied in order to enable the students to flourish.[3] The autistic teacher, well aware of their own struggles and the challenges that are brought to learning in neurotypical environments, is able to foster a space that encourages the least of those students amongst the class. The least are not necessarily those who are judged as academically incapable but the least are those that, in the eyes of normative theological pedagogies more likely to suffer inequality and lack of access to life giving theology that should be available to them. For example, typical measures of achievement such as an essay written linear, progressive argumentation might normally receive good marks for a theological assignment, yet for an autistic student may not reflect the way that they learn. Hannah Lewis (2021, p. 7) in her liberative theology for d/Deaf people suggests that notions of academic validity prejudice people who sign to communicate, for example. The autistic experience of knowing, as indicated, does not always match notions of academic validity. Thus the autistic teacher can facilitate the legitimization of non-linear, non-normative ways of expressing knowing—for example in the formation of assessments that do not valorize argumentation as a form of knowledge production. Such assessments, if they need exist at all, could be creative, artistic, first-person accounts or freely constructed alongside the individual to account for their preferred communication methods. The autistic teacher of theology opens the way to this theology in the manner of a priest as they facilitate access, show the way, enable the postures and bodily positions that are worshipful and alongside the student in their learning about and with God and the church. The autistic teacher facilitates the testimonies of the autistic student by creating spaces that allow for the stories of God to be shared in whichever way is appropriate for that student so that their experience of the divine is afforded time and recognition.

How can such testimony be given and received in a way that is constructive and importantly, *safe*, for those that offer it? Slee (2020) advocates that the theological educators are persistent learners engaged in scholarship. This means that they "incarnate" the subject for the students (Slee, 2020, p. 176). How much more is this the case for those students who look to the autistic theological educator as an example of someone who goes before them, travels alongside them and uniquely corresponds to their own lived experiences. The autistic teacher is therefore prophetic in their embodied presence in the classroom, one who, in seeking to make theological education a "saving work" following Rebecca Chopp they do so by their very presence (Chopp, 1995). This counters the absence of autistic voices and presence in the first instance, allowing for modeling and presence to facilitate students' giving of their own testimony or being present in their own spaces. To counter the testimonial injustice that says autistic people are examples of the inability of humanity to connect with the divine, the embodied presence of an autistic person in the theological academy illustrates the counter-narrative. Epistemological justice is found in their presence, one who opens the way toward a plurality of theological knowings and travels alongside autistic students in mutuality, holding lightly decisions of concrete and approved knowledge and being open to different ways and descriptions of theological information.

Curriculum – in the light of Pentecost

Willie James Jennings describes "whiteness" as,

A way of being in the world and seeing the world that forms cognitive and affective structures able to seduce people into its habitation its meaning making. (Jennings, 2020, p. 9)

This form of being in the world homogenizes difference not according to ethnic white European people per se but by the attitude of uniformity of the academy that is white, self-sufficient masculinity (Jennings, 2020, p. 6). For the purposes of an autistic theology this uniformity can be said to oppress diverse knowing and silence the value and power of lived experiences. It is neurotypical theology. The lived experiences of autistic people have little role in the doctrinal and biblical propositional theology of the academy and are not brought to bear in theologizing for autistic lives.

Jesus spoke to Peter in the district of Caesarea Philippi and said to him "But who do you say that I am?" (Matthew 16.15). Peter, having accounted for all the other ideas and identities that those around him claimed, identified Jesus as the Messiah. It has long been important for theology to speak rightly about God and to identify the Messiah correctly. However, the noise of multiple claims to rightness—to proper knowledge—eclipses the straightforward and the confessional. The autistic person is identified in the literature as one who cannot possibly know God, or if they do, imperfectly and with deficit. This, for example, is illustrated in Stump (2010, pp. 64–82) where autism is considered deficit, autistics are unable to "mind read" and therefore know people and this is correlated to ability to know God. A curriculum that requires students to adopt such propositions and the rigid theologies that accommodate them do not allow for a liberative curriculum. Rather, a theology that encompasses the reality of humanity in light of Pentecost, where the Spirit can baptize all flesh and all types of flesh, takes a different and more embracing view of curriculum.

> The practice of ministry in new and previously unexplored contexts should return us to the rest of the curriculum with fresh hermeneutical and methodological considerations. (Yong, 2020, p. 96)

Yong claims that the contextuality of the post-Pentecost theologies that realizes the value of students in all walks of life allows for the reinterpretation of curriculums. Curriculums that are post-colonial, post-modern, rejecting of the self-sufficiency of the individual and corporate in worship and learning lean strongly against the "whiteness" of the theological curriculum of old and embrace novel ways of God-knowing.

Eunjoo Mary Kim writes of the flaws in Christian doctrine that rely upon social norms to describe the image of God. God is omnipotent, perfect, whole and autonomous (Kim, 2020). Even the author of Leviticus, she argues, believed God was like this and therefore the priests who represent him should also be so. All "imperfection" must be eliminated if approaching God is your vocation.

Based on this understanding, the traditional Christian view believes that the image of God is an individual property given by God as human nature at the time of creation, and which presents the standard of social normalcy – an able body, reason, and the ability to be in a relationship with God and other human beings. (Kim, 2020 pp. 34–35)

The problem with such renderings of God is that many theologians themselves, never mind the students, do not meet the standards to represent God's image. Such theologies become "disabling theologies" (Eiesland, 1994, p. 69). Disabling theologies, as described by Nancy L. Eiesland, are the theologies that cause shame and damage. Examples of such are those theologies that associate sin with disability or, as shown above, theologies that associate autism with inability to access God. Eiesland comments that not only do these theologies cause harm, they do not represent those about whom they speak, their lived reality and their experience (Eiesland, 1994, p. 70). The alternative to such epistemic injustice and the theologies that facilitate it is conscientization.

Conscientization, or critical consciousness, is Freire's theory that rejects knowledge deposited into the minds of knowers. Education that collaborates with controlling and dominant powers, that places its trust in systems that further oppressions, this education relies upon authorized knowledge, approved descriptions and doctrines that oppressed being transferred to students to repeat the systems that cause harm. Pedagogy based on critical consciousness seeks to transform reality by allowing those who are oppressed to see the reality of their situation for themselves. This is not achieved by putting different information into their minds, but by recognizing their own reality and historical situation. It is furthered by dialogue, and for theology dialogue that incorporates hope (Parker, 2022, p. 164). As I've already shown, this can be also theologized as realizing the reality of the nature of salvation for all flesh. Such a curriculum that recognizes historical particularity and salvation history necessitates the autistic student to be facilitated toward recognizing their own situation.

Toward peculiar pedagogies of Christian education

Autistic theological students and theological educators are participants in systems for their formation that do not account for their lived experience and do not facilitate their flourishing. This article has argued that the naming of autistic oppression in higher education should be called epistemic injustice. That this injustice denies the lived and bodily knowing of autistic people and perpetuates systems that fail to recognize autistic people and cast them as examples of poor relationships with God, people in need of a cure and metaphors of selfishness. Autistic people need, therefore, to experience Freire's conscientization, the awareness that they are human subjects who are victims of this oppressive theological descriptions. Theological education needs to take seriously the challenge of liberative pedagogies.

Suggestions for how this might occur through a theological lens are reforming the classroom as having levelness regarding knowledge. Practically classrooms can facilitate movement for autistic bodies that do not wish to sit still, acknowledging a coming and going can still allow for learning. Issues of sound, lighting, temperature and seating should all be considered contingent—each individual autistic person has specific needs and requirements for access and these can be discussed. It may be as simple, such as in my experience of teaching, as allowing the student to sit at the back with permission to leave if need be. Interruptions and verbal ticks can be understood as contributions rather than rudeness or inappropriate engagement. Indeed, communication itself typically understood as written and analytical in order to be assessed and graded could be reconsidered. What way can an autistic person's knowledge of God and the texts of the faithful be assessed? For the verbose autistic, an oral assessment might suit. For the non-speaking autistic then a written assessment with a good deal of additional time and the presence of facilitators could be allowed. Typically such variations of assessments are prohibited, even considered cheating, by validating authorities but it is such systems that prevent access to non-conforming autistic knowledge.

All knowledge is both gained, generated and transferred by equal partners in the learning context. This is examined theologically through the biblical story of Babel, the gift of speaking in tongues and autistic relationships with speech. The teacher or lecturer has a role as one who holds the class before God in a holy space, in the manner of a priest and a prophet. The curriculum focuses on the liberative potential innate in theology, focused by the path of critical consciousness raising and orientated against those theologies which damage and harm autistic lives.

Notes

1. Milton (2012). For the most significant challenge to the notion that autistic people are 'failures' at necessary social interactions.
2. For a more developed version of this argument see Williams (2023), Peculiar Discipleship: An Autistic Liberation Theology SCM Press.
3. Slee is clear that this is not in the manner of powerlessness but the teacher has a strong and firm sense of their own identity rooted in Christ. See page 173

Disclosure statement

No potential conflict of interest was reported by the authors.

References

Biklen, D., & Attfield, R. (Eds.). (2005). *Autism and the myth of the person alone*. New York University Press.

Chapman, R., & Carel, H. (2022). Neurodiversity, epistemic injustice, and the good human life. *Journal of Social Philosophy*, *53*(4), 614–631. https://doi.org/10.1111/josp.12456

Chopp, R. S. (1995). *Saving work: Feminist practices of theological education* (1st ed). Westminster John Knox Press.

Cohn, Eli G., Keith R. McVilly, Matthew J. Harrison, and Lillian N. Stiegler. Repeating Purposefully: Empowering Educators with Functional Communication Models of Echolalia in Autism. *Autism & Developmental Language Impairments, 7* (January 2022): 239694152210919. https://doi.org/10.1177/23969415221091928

Cornwall, S., Clare-Young, A., & Gillingham, S. (2022). Epistemic injustice exacerbating trauma in Christian theological treatments of trans people and people with intersex characteristics. In K. O'Donnell & K. Cross (Eds.), *Bearing witness: Intersectional perspectives on trauma theology* (pp. 111–130). SCM Press.

Dinishak, J., & Akhtar, N. (2023). Integrating autistic perspectives into autism science: A role for autistic autobiographies. *Autism : The International Journal of Research and Practice*, *27*(3), 578–587. https://doi.org/10.1177/13623613221123731

Eiesland, N. L. (1994). *The disabled god: Toward a liberatory theology of disability*. Abingdon Press.

Freire, P. (2017). *Pedagogy of the oppressed* (M. Bergman Ramos, Trans.; Published in Penguin Classics 2017). Penguin Books.

Fricker, M. (2011). *Epistemic injustice: Power and the ethics of knowing (REPR)*. Oxford University Press.

Gates, Gordon S. (2019). *Trauma, stigma and autism: Developing resilience and loosening the grip of shame*. London; Philadelphia: Jessica Kingsley Publishers.

Jennings, W. J. (2020). *After whiteness: An education in belonging*. William B. Eerdmans Publishing Company.

Johns, C. B. (2010). *Pentecostal formation: A pedagogy among the oppressed*. Wipf & Stock.

Kim, E. M. (2020). Sacramental preaching in the culture of ableism. *Liturgy*, *35*(3), 32–37. https://doi.org/10.1080/0458063X.2020.1796441

Lewis, H. (2021). *Deaf liberation theology*. Routledge.

Limburg, J. (2021). *Letters to my weird sisters*. Atlantic Books.

Macaskill, G. (2021). *Autism and the church: Bible, theology, and community (First issued in paperback)*. Baylor University Press.

Macaskill, G. (2022). The Bible, autism and other profound developmental conditions: Regulating hermeneutics. *Journal of Disability & Religion*, *26*(4), 414–438. https://doi.org/10.1080/23312521.2021.1881024

Macchia, F. D. (2012). Babel and the tongues of Pentecost: reversal or fulfilment? In M. J. Cartledge (Ed.), *Speaking in tongues multi-disciplinary perspectives* (pp. 34–51). Wipf and Stock Publishers.

McFall, M. T. (2022). Divine hiddenness and spiritual autism. *The Heythrop Journal*, *63*(4), 757–769. https://doi.org/10.1111/heyj.12324

Milton, D. E. M. (2012). On the ontological status of autism: The 'double empathy problem'. *Disability & Society*, *27*(6), 883–887. https://doi.org/10.1080/09687599.2012.710008

Parker, E. (2022). *Trust in theological education: Deconstructing 'trustworthiness' for a pedagogy of liberation*. SCM Press.

Pinder-Amaker, S. (2014). Identifying the unmet needs of college students on the autism spectrum. *Harvard Review of Psychiatry*, *22*(2), 125–137. https://doi.org/10.1097/HRP.0000000000000032

Rapley, S. (2021). *Autistic thinking in the life of the church*. SCM PRESS.

Reddie, A. G. (2023). Transformative, Christian religious education and praxis forms of learning. In A. Cocksworth, R. Starr, & S. Burns (Eds.), *From the shores of silence: Conversations in feminist practical theology* (pp. 196–211). SCM Press.

Slee, N. (2020). *Fragments for fractured times: What feminist practical theology brings to the table.* SCM Press.

Stump, E. (2010). Narrative and the knowledge of persons. In E. Stump (Ed.), *Wandering in darkness* (1st ed., pp. 64–82). Oxford University Press. https://doi.org/10.1093/acprof:Oso/9780199277421.003.0004

Van Ommen, A. L., & Endress, T. (2022). Reframing liturgical theology through the lens of autism: A qualitative study of autistic experiences of worship. *Studia Liturgica, 52*(2), 219–234. https://doi.org/10.1177/00393207221111573

Waldock, K. E., & Forrester-Jones, R. (2020). An exploratory study of attitudes toward autism amongst church-going Christians in the South East of England, United Kingdom. *Journal of Disability & Religion, 24*(4), 349–370. https://doi.org/10.1080/23312521.2020.1776667

Williams, C. (2022). Autism: An autoethnography of a peculiar trauma. In K. O'Donnell & K. Cross (Eds.), *Bearing witness: Intersectional perspectives on trauma theology* (pp. 187–204). SCM Press.

Williams, C. (2023). *Peculiar discipleship: An autistic liberation theology.* SCM Press.

Yong, A. (2020). *Renewing the church by the spirit: Theological education after Pentecost.* William B. Eerdmans Publishing Company.

ad OPEN ACCESS

United by Neurodiversity: Postgraduate Research in a Neurodiverse Context

Armand Léon van Ommen, Henna J. Cundill, Krysia Emily Waldock, Catherine Tryfona, Grant Macaskill, Christopher Barber, Sarah Douglas, Bryan W. Fowler, Harry Gibbins, Ian Lasch and Brian Brock

ABSTRACT

This article contributes to the discussion of neurodiversity and theological education by presenting a self-reflection by a group of researchers affiliated with the Centre for Autism and Theology at the University of Aberdeen. Literature on postgraduates' experiences is missing from the current discussion on neurodiversity in higher education. This article offers first-hand accounts as a start to address this gap in the literature. Through the self-reflection exercise, it became clear how this group goes beyond policy documents on equality, diversity, and inclusion (EDI) by embodying what it means to be a neurodiverse group and what working together looks like in practice. This was characterized by the following themes: all are valued, students feel well-supported, and space for multiple perspectives enabled challenging the status quo in churches, theology, and the wider autism discourse. Theologically, the group interpreted their experiences along the images of the body of Christ and the *imago Dei*.

Introduction

This article contributes to the discussion of neurodiversity and theological education by presenting a self-reflection by a group of researchers affiliated with the Centre for Autism and Theology (CAT) at the University of Aberdeen. The Centre aims to be an international and interdisciplinary hub for research on autism and theology. Throughout the academic year, a neurodiverse[1] group of postgraduate students and academic staff from Aberdeen and other universities gather weekly to discuss articles, book chapters, their own writing, or a specific theme of common interest. The neurodivergences include mainly autism, but also ADHD, dyslexia, dyspraxia, and possibly more. Typically, slightly over half of the people

This is an Open Access article distributed under the terms of the Creative Commons Attribution License (http://creativecommons.org/licenses/by/4.0/), which permits unrestricted use, distribution, and reproduction in any medium, provided the original work is properly cited. The terms on which this article has been published allow the posting of the Accepted Manuscript in a repository by the author(s) or with their consent.

gathered for any one meeting identify as neurodivergent; the others identify as neurotypical. The focus of the discussions is usually on autism, as the group comes under the purview of the Centre for Autism and Theology.[2]

To our knowledge, the Centre is a unique platform for bringing together an international, interdisciplinary, and intentionally neurodiverse group of researchers who are all interested in autism (or other forms of neurodivergence), theology, and church. Through the self-reflection exercise, it became clear that this group goes beyond ticking the boxes of policy documents on equality, diversity, and inclusion (EDI); it *embodies* what it means to be a neurodiverse group and what working together looks like in practice. Furthermore, rather than privileging either neurodivergent or neurotypical voices, the Centre for Autism and Theology explicitly encourages dialog across neurotypes. The wider autism discourse has historically, and sometimes is still, divided between the voices of (neurotypical) parents and/or researchers on the one hand, and autistic people on the other. At the Centre, we are convinced that the discourse needs both, and to put it in theological terms, that reconciliation between these groups is needed.[3] This group of researchers seems to be unique in the way that they embody these values—at least, those involved in the group say that it provides a sense of acceptance, safety, and valuing of neurodivergent voices that they seldom find elsewhere. It should be emphasized here, however, that members are invited to participate based on their common interest in autism and theology rather than because of their specific neurotype. It is perhaps this shared interest that facilitates dialogue and brings about reflection within the group, where the voices of both neurodivergent and neurotypical people are shared and considered in an open and welcoming environment. Where differences emerge, these are regarded as opportunities to share experiences and foster greater understanding.

Therefore, it was proposed that an in-depth self-reflection would be a worthwhile contribution to this issue on neurodiversity and theological education. The purpose of this article is not to evaluate the group's practices against the Centre's values but to show how one group of researchers tries to embody the values of in-depth, mutual listening across neurotypes, strengthening each other's research, and valuing each person's voice and experiences with regards to the discourses and practices surrounding autism and faith. In this, the values of the Centre and those held by the group's members overlap. By presenting this self-reflection exercise, we do not intend to provide a blueprint for other groups, but we trust that other groups might take inspiration from this example, and apply what is relevant to their own context.

Our self-reflection focuses on the experience of being researchers in a neurodiverse research context or group and how we might reflect on this theologically. In what follows, we briefly explain our method for this reflection exercise. We then present the themes that emerged from the reflection exercise. The last of these themes concerns theological reflection in particular.

Methods

Inherent to the topic of neurodiversity are multiple perspectives. This is our experience at the Centre for Autism and Theology, and to enable every group member to participate in the process of writing this article, the following method was designed. First, we held early discussions in the group to review existing literature on autistic experiences of higher education (of which there is a dearth[4]) and to formulate questions to guide our self-reflection:

1. What is the experience (practically or otherwise) of studying, supervising, researching, and interacting with researchers (students and staff) in the neurodiverse context of the Centre for Autism and Theology?
2. How do CAT members reflect on this experience theologically—in other words, what does neurodiversity (in the context of CAT) bring to the study of theology?

All of the group members were invited to write a personal response of ~500 words to these two questions and send them to the first author. Responding in this way was taken to be an indication that one wanted to contribute to this article and to the further process of collaborating on it. These responses were then sent to those group members who had written a response (not everybody chose to participate). These participating group members ($n = 8$) were asked to identify common themes across the responses. The group members were then invited to a meeting to discuss the themes that had been identified. Due to the timing (Holy Week in the Western Christian tradition) and short deadlines, only four people could attend the meeting, although two others had sent the themes that they had identified beforehand so that those themes could be included in the discussion. The analyses of the group members were remarkably similar. One member had created a visual representation of the themes that she had identified, which covered most of the themes identified by others. After refining that visual representation in light of the analyses of the group members, this became the basis for writing the Themes section below. Two group members sent their responses after this meeting, but these confirmed our analysis and did not add new elements.

The first author wrote a first draft and sent that to the three members who were present at the meeting. They provided feedback, which the first author integrated into the article, which was then circulated to all participants for comment. In this way, the article reflects a whole group collaboration. The final version includes feedback from the editors of this journal issue and the anonymous peer feedback.

The method that we designed to write this article has a few limitations. First, a collective self-reflection may not have the same "status" as a research article. For example, if an independent researcher had conducted interviews with the group members, they might have found slightly different themes—perhaps including more negative responses that participants would have felt more comfortable to give anonymously. However, given the dearth of research on the experience of autistic researchers, and especially *postgraduate* students, we consider the format of a self-reflection project to be a worthwhile contribution to the small body of existing research, because it foregrounds the experience of a group that is intentionally neurodiverse and that makes neurodivergent perspectives central.[5] Second, as a collective self-reflection, it will become clear in this article that all the researchers currently involved identify as Christian and/or work within a Christian framework. That does not mean that the group would not welcome people of other faiths and religions, on the contrary, it is simply a reflection of the current constellation of the group. Finally, given that the first author, who is also the supervisor of a number of the students that contributed to this article, took the lead in organizing this self-reflection and drafted the first version of this article, one may critically note the power dynamics inherent in this set up. We acknowledge these dynamics. Again, at this point an independent researcher might have gotten additional or different comments and reflections from the group members. Whilst we cannot put aside the power dynamics entirely, Sarah (an Aberdeen Master of Theology by Research student who identifies as autistic) commented: "I have noticed that the attitude amongst the research community at CAT is one of generosity, a willingness to share research ideas and mutually supportive. Supervisors encourage and are appreciative of student reviews of their work and this as well as the CAT and PT [= Practical Theology] meetings have a sense of democracy and respect underpinning them." Other responses echo Sarah's observation, as will become clear throughout this article.

Themes

Four main themes emerged from our individual analyses and subsequent discussion. The first theme is "All are valued" and includes three sub-themes: "All-embracing community," "Neurodiverse conversations," and "Sensitivity to power in landscape." The other themes are "Well-supported," "Challenging the status quo," and "Theological framework." All themes are related to each other, but we will highlight some specific relationships between the themes that are particularly noteworthy.

All are valued

One theme that stands out across all responses to the two questions is that the group members feel that every participant is valued in the Centre for Autism and Theology's research group. Not only is each member valued as a person, but their disciplinary perspectives or theological differences are also valued. As discussed below, this ethos has a theological underpinning, which gives it additional force (see "Theological framework").

Various (autistic) group members contrast this welcoming ethos with previous experiences of other groups, including churches. Harry (an Aberdeen PhD student who identifies as autistic) notes:

> People belong [in churches] only on certain conditions in which belonging becomes a reward for adherence to a moral code. What is clear from the plethora of research undertaken by members of the Centre of Autism and Theology is that it is this misguided apprehension of difference that is to be addressed within the context of being an autistic person.

He also speaks about the need to "mask" differences to adhere to a community's norms and belong. Many autistic (or otherwise (neuro)divergent) people "mask" or "camouflage" (Cook et al., 2021). Sarah speaks about this in relation to her studies as an undergraduate student quite a few years ago. At the time, she did not know she was autistic. Despite "muddling through" she achieved good grades, "albeit at a huge cost to my mental, spiritual and physical health and a vow to never to pick up an academic book again." Other differences can be equally difficult to navigate. For example, one might do research on a religious topic in a social science context, where that topic is not always understood or appreciated by colleagues. In the words of one researcher: "I feel people in spaces that share the same interests and passions as me will always end up being more fruitful than places where I cannot be authentic." As a research group, we try to value differences and all disciplinary perspectives, hoping that all members feel that they can be authentic and valued. The following subthemes provide more texture as to how we try to live this ethos.

All-embracing community

Whilst research on neurodivergence unites the group, the members' positionalities differ significantly. Consequently, it is accurate to describe the group as "all-embracing" as to acknowledge the variety of member's experiences. It is not simply that each person's contribution is valued, but a recognition that their lived experience is unique, is to be embraced, and that it enriches the conversation. Most members are theologians, but the group includes social scientists and a computing scientist, and some join as theologians but also have degrees in other disciplines. Some are ordained clergy. Various members identify as autistic or otherwise neurodivergent, but some are neurotypical. Some are parents of neurodivergent children (this is true for both autistic and non-autistic group members). Regarding sex and gender, the group is fairly balanced.[6] The group ranges in age from early twenties to sixties with a good balance between decades. Usually, most people who join the weekly meetings are students, but various academic staff members from different universities, including the University of Aberdeen, are part of the group. Group members come from various countries, although less diversity is found when it comes to ethnicity.

Finally, some members can see each other in person, especially those staff and students based in Aberdeen, other students join for the annual Postgraduate Research Symposium in Aberdeen, whilst yet others only know each other through virtual interactions. Being a distance student is a "double-edged sword," as Chris (an Aberdeen PhD student who identifies as autistic) explains: "[O]n the one side being a distant learning student can be very isolating and lonely whilst on the other I value the solitude inherent in being a distant learning student, my space where I do not have to perform or engage socially if I do not want to." As all these differences show, this research group is indeed an all-embracing community, but a community nevertheless, for which it is even more significant that each person and positionality is valued.

Neurodiverse conversations and communication

Such an all-embracing community, with its ethos of valuing and welcoming each other, creates a unique context for conversations between and across neurotypes. Several autistic members commented in their responses that they feel that they can more easily be themselves in this group than in some other groups that they are part of because approximately half of the group members identify as autistic or as neurodivergent in some other way. In the words of Ian (a PhD student who identifies as autistic):

> While I was greatly looking forward to my studies, it never occurred to me that I would find community along the way (in part because I've only ever felt tangentially connected, at best, to other communities I've ostensibly been a part of). Finding a place and a group of people where I feel as though I belong has been a great source of learning, and even beyond that, of joy.

Ian comments that he feels understood by the group, partly because of having autistic peers in the group but also due to the understanding of autism that non-autistic group members share. Harry comments about this understanding too:

> CAT helps me to be myself because I get to whittle endlessly about theology and how much I love it. They take me seriously when I speak for the eighteenth time about how *Dungeons and Dragons* can be a theological tool for understanding creativity and storytelling. They do not tell me to stay on topic if I begin telling them niche trivia about *Doctor Who*. Instead, I am free to the creative, explorative, and formative process of theological study at a pace and a tone which make sense to me.

It seems that the people in this group feel more free to contribute to the conversation than might be the case in other settings. The result is a level of authenticity that is necessary for good research, as Krysia (a PhD student at another university) commented. They also speak about conversations across neurotypes: "I have personally had a variety of stimulating discussions with colleagues who identify as neurodivergent, and those who do not. I enjoy the quality of interaction I have with autistic colleagues, but also deeply value the neurodiverse conversations with non-autistic identifying peers."

At the same time, neurotypicals also value being part of a neurodiverse community, where they can regularly check their understanding and interpretation of autism. Henna (an Aberdeen PhD student who identifies as neurotypical) commented:

> The regular contact means that my research and writing is embedded in an ongoing process of feedback and refinement, which helps me to avoid pathologizing neurodivergence or making assumptions based on my own experience of the world. I value getting feedback both from those with first person, lived experience of being autistic/neurodivergent, but also from those who are in caring roles, as I have often found these two perspectives to be quite different.

Similarly, Léon (Aberdeen academic staff who identifies as neurotypical), wrote in his response:

> For me, as a non-autistic supervisor working in the area of autism and supervising autistic students, it is a hugely enriching experience to spend much time with autistic students and academic staff. Through my contact with all these students and researchers, I learn much about autism, including how it works out in the lives of people on a daily basis. This helps to go beyond stereotypes and to see each person for who they are.

These conversations across neurotypes help to improve our own writing and publications, in part because they elicit feedback from this group of researchers that (mostly) study similar topics. Discussing work in progress with those who identify as neurodivergent in various ways helps to expose where such work is being unconsciously governed (and weakened) by the assumptive world of one particular viewpoint. The non-autistic researcher gains the viewpoint of the autistic researcher, and vice-versa, as to how various theological propositions might be heard and understood by those who think differently, and how proposals related to the Christian life might work out in practice. In this way, our discussions help to mitigate issues arising due to the double empathy problem. The double empathy problem states that the communication partners better understand communication between members of the same neurotype, as well as each other's experience of the world, than when the conversation takes place across neurotypes (Milton, 2012). Discussing our research in a neurodiverse group allows researchers to engage "in an ongoing process of feedback and refinement." Also, too often misunderstanding between autistic and non-autistic people has caused alienation and pain. Reconciliation is needed; the research group embodies this.

Sensitivity to power in landscape

Weekly conversations about neurodiversity inevitably lead to discussions of masking (as noted above), fitting in, marginalization, and power dynamics. Autistic people often feel like a stranger in a world in which the social rules seem self-evident to everyone else. This is sometimes illustrated by the analogy of visiting a country in which you do not speak the language. Inevitably, that leads to social exclusion, insecurity, anxiety, and awkward situations (see e.g., Rapley, 2021, pp. 27–28). To fit in, autistic people feel they need to adapt to the social norms and "mask" their own autistic behavior and thinking (Miller et al., 2021; Sedgewick et al., 2022). It is clear how this leads to power imbalances. The conversations in our group make us more aware of these dynamics in the context of the academy, church, and wider society. These conversations also form us as researchers and as human beings, in turn shaping our research. One example of this is that there is a keen sense in the group that research about autism should be done in consultation with autistic people, leading some students and staff to use methodologies that suit that way of working. This includes the use of Participatory Action Research, a method of enquiry in which researchers and stakeholders work collaboratively to gain an understanding of a situation or phenomenon, with a view to implementing a positive process of change (Cameron et al., 2010). Another researcher within the group is using creative ways to include autistic people within the design of their research (e.g., critical friends, see Kember et al., 1997) to "tap into" reflexivity of their own social position and identities. Another example is that this awareness helps us to keep in view the question of how our research will benefit neurodivergent people. We will return to this subtheme when discussing the themes of "Challenging the status quo" and "Theological framework." For now, it suffices to say that the conversations in the research group help to readdress the power imbalance, and hopefully provide a space safe enough so that masking is not necessary.

Well-supported

The second theme follows from the first, and from its subthemes: group members report that they feel well-supported. Being valued *as you are* is arguably a form of support in itself. In addition, some group members made specific comments about the support that they experienced from being part of the Centre for Autism and Theology's research community. For example, students feel that their supervisors are knowledgeable about autism. Supervisors are not perfect, but students see and appreciate that they do the best that they can to support their autistic (and other) students, including trying to understand what it means to be an autistic researcher.

Another form of support that both staff members and students receive from being part of this research community is related to the specific constellation of the group (see "All-embracing community" above): theologians in the group benefit from the input of other disciplinary perspectives and vice versa. Each discipline has its own paradigm, and having conversations across those paradigms as well as listening to debates in a discipline other than one's own sharpens our research. Such discussions can be fruitful in our context, where everyone feels valued and where there is a common focus and interest in autism, church, and theology.

Challenging the status quo

Two defining characteristics of the Centre for Autism and Theology give the research that emerges from the Centre a particular outlook that challenges the status quo in theology and other disciplines. First, the research group is keen to do research *with* autistic people and encourages autistic researchers to embrace their positionality as being autistic, reflecting on how that plays out in their research. Moreover, the group encourages non-autistic members also to be aware of their positionality as non-autistic which is again related to the double-empathy problem that we mentioned above (Waldock & Keates, 2022). Second, the Centre takes a non-pathological approach to autism, which means that autism is not seen primarily as a disorder, but as a particular way of being in the world, which can result in unique experiences and perspectives. That is not to say that the group takes a dismissive approach to the challenges that autistic people may face, but it questions whether those challenges are always inherent to autism, or are a function of the way society and communities are structured. To be sure, the researchers in this group do not agree on all aspects of how to evaluate the medical, social, or other models of disability. However, these two characteristics of the Centre for Autism and Theology do give a certain perspective on autism and how autism relates to theological discussions.

The centrality of autistic people themselves in our research projects, and the non-pathological approach that we encourage, result in critical questions that the research group brings to the table in theological discussions more broadly. These relate to faith communities and their practices, and to the academic discourse around autism. In the words of Grant (an Aberdeen staff member who identifies as autistic): "To work in a group where autistic leadership is recognized, such that the 'normalcy' of the neurotypical is never presumed, itself frames the issues in very different ways to most contexts." For example, Bryan (an Aberdeen PhD student who identifies as non-autistic) notes how "our readings and discussions at the Centre for Autism and Theology have shaped my theological thinking, giving me insights that I would not have received from my [church] tradition and enabling me to see the world the way God sees it." In a similar vein, Henna comments:

> Within my own project it has become apparent how much existing theology is (to quote one of my research participants) "neurotypically coded" – i.e., it assumes a neurotypical experience of language, cognitive/physical wellbeing, social profile/preferences. It has highlighted to me how much 'spiritual scorekeeping' is centered around practices which are essentially social, e.g., weekly church attendance or vocalized extempore prayer.

One means by which these new perspectives are gained, and in which questions are raised, is through the specific interest that theology has in how language functions to describe but also to construct realities. Hence attention is given by various group members to the language we use around autism (Macaskill, 2019, pp. 9–10; Van Ommen, 2023, pp. 22–29). At the same time, given that an estimated 25–35% of autistic people do not use spoken language as their primary way of communication (i.e., they are non- or minimally speaking; see Norrelgen et al., 2015; Russell et al., 2019) the perspective of this autistic sub-group provides yet another important angle from which to consider the (theological) questions that the research group tries to discern and to address.

Attention to language, dehumanizing theories of autism, power dynamics, and more, questions the "normalcy" that is operant in most academic, religious, and societal contexts. In that regard, the research group benefits from being embedded in the Divinity department at the University of Aberdeen, with a longstanding practice of paying attention to those who are marginalized by society because of disabilities, mental health challenges, dementia, or otherwise. The research group provides an opportunity to "practice what we preach" in terms of becoming a community where each person is valued and belongs. Living the vision of what we preach, however imperfectly, has the potential to challenge the status quo beyond mere policy documents on Equality, Diversity, and Inclusion.

Theological framework

The fourth theme, "Theological framework," can be seen as the theme that underpins all of the above. In the responses that the group members wrote to the two initial questions, the theological underpinning was particularly evident in the reflections on how "All are valued." As noted in the discussion of that theme, the theological underpinning gives additional force to the welcome that the group gives to each member and the valuing of multiple perspectives, because that ethos is not just a social nicety but is in fact deeply rooted in the theological notion that God values all people. It was remarkable that many members referred to St. Paul's image of the body of Christ (1 Cor. 12:12-31) and applied that to how the research group functions. The group members, especially those who identify as autistic, seem to find a place where they feel that they can fit in and belong, in ways that they do not always experience in other places. In the words of Grant: "The biblical image of the body is not intended to convey the complexity of anatomy, but the vitality of physiology, of a body that lives because it has lots of different parts." The research group is a place where in some small way St. Paul's image is embodied.

There is a prophetic edge to the Pauline image of the body of Christ that we often blunt unwittingly, a disruptive challenge to value each part of the body, particularly those parts that wider society and the academy often functionally regard as "weaker." Ian wrote in his response:

> I have long considered Paul's language of the Body of Christ to be much more than just metaphor, and I think this is a part of what's been missing sometimes from experiences of Christian community that I have found before. If we really are going to value every member of the Body, and for the unique part that it happens to be, then I think that we need to have a much greater appreciation for diversity *per se* than it seems to me most Christian communities, including higher education communities, do.

In a similar vein, Léon wrote:

> Autistic people have too often been excluded from church (and society and academy). The hand has said to the foot too often that it didn't need the foot. CAT

provides a platform or context in which autistic researchers and their allies are encouraged to take their rightful place in the body of Christ – academically and otherwise – and even to show the hand that it was wrong in thinking it didn't need the foot.

Chris, reflecting on what he brings to the table as an autistic researcher, sums up this prophetic approach nicely when he writes that he brings his "ability and calling to be a dreamer and a fighter." We should note that the research group meetings are not an exercise in being critical of church, theology, or the academy. Out of a position of being marginalized as neurodivergent people, and as neurotypicals trying to be good allies, it is inevitable that the pain and disappointment of being marginalized is shared in our discussions. All members, however, are also appreciative of initiatives by various communities, including the church and the academy, that support neurodivergent people to reach their full potential. The discussions in the group and the research undertaken emerge out of a passion to see God's reign breaking into the various contexts of which we are part. Naturally, that means being critical where needed, but only because many in the group would echo Chris' self-description of being "fighters and dreamers."

Other theological images or notions provide further underpinning to the research and ethics of the group. In particular, the notion of being created in the image of God is important to various group members. Bryan reflects: "Moreover, CAT has demonstrated how my theological tradition has often failed to consider the diversity of others' ways of thinking and being. I have found it disturbing to hear from some in my tradition who do not acknowledge that a person bears God's image because of a diagnosis or neurodiversity." Similarly reflecting on diversity and the image of God, Sarah writes:

> Theology, like church communities, needs neurodivergence to inform, challenge and enrich its neuro-normative systems of belief, dogma and praxis. It needs different minds and ways of experiencing the world, faith and belonging in dialogue with respectful non-autistic academics to inclusively broaden its relevance and representation of what it means to be human and made in the image of God.

Obviously, the notion of diversity is included in the body of Christ image, and it is interesting to see how some group members connect this also to being created in the image of God. Hands, feet, and all other parts are needed in the body of Christ—are needed to do good theology— together reflecting the image of God, as body of Christ, who is the image of God (Macaskill, 2019, pp. 93–97).

Finally, under this theme, we should state the perhaps obvious yet unique feature of the Centre for Autism and Theology's research group, which is the space it creates for the interplay between autism and theology.

All the research projects that the group members conduct have neurodiversity or a particular neurodivergence as their focus (mostly autism). These projects are approached theologically, or when set in another disciplinary context religion is in view. Moreover, the research questions are addressed through an autistic lens—where the researcher is neurotypical, they go to great lengths to adopt an autistic lens to whatever extent that is possible. This will result in an increasing number of publications that can be classified either as autistic theologies or theologies of autism (and possibly autistic theologies of autism). At the same time, the theological context of the group results in theological perspectives on autism, providing a unique disciplinary perspective to the wider autism discourse. As theologians, we can reflect on what it means for autistic people to be created in the image of God or to function, as a group, as the body of Christ, in ways that would be beyond the scope of other disciplines.

Conclusion

On the surface, one sees a small group of researchers who meet weekly to chat, drink coffee, share their works-in-progress, and discuss the various topics and questions that arise from their research. However, that same group embodies the aspiration for equality, diversity, and inclusion (EDI) that is written into policy documents, showing that documents in itself are not enough—EDI is only a reality when it is embodied. Part of that embodiment is the intentional mutual cooperation between, and listening across, neurotypes, living the kind of reconciliation between different voices and experiences that the Centre for Autism and Theology seeks to promote—values that are shared by the group's members. This reconciliation was recognized in one image this group used in this self-reflection exercise: "the body of Christ"—in which no preferential treatment or exclusion is conferred on stronger or weaker members. As our thematic analysis has identified, members feel that their contribution is welcomed and valued, regardless of their neurotype, age, or status within the academy. This contributes to the well-being of group members, especially those who may feel excluded from some other social facets of university life. Moreover, different disciplines and research interests are brought to the table each week. This not only enriches the research but enriches the researchers, creating opportunities to explore different perspectives on the work that they do.

Although we seek not to give a list of recommendations or a "tick list," in terms of what other groups might seek to embed from our approach, an intentionality surrounding acceptance and reflection on the social position each individual occupies is key. A list of recommendations could be applied in an insensitive manner with an output expected. Furthermore, our critical reflection highlights the importance of our theological standpoint, which in many ways grounds and shapes how our group works. Where "normative modes of belonging" within church spaces have been critiqued (Waldock, 2023), perhaps the same questions remain of how appropriate a goal of "being inclusive" is in theological education spaces. However much of an oxymoron it may sound, it is no exaggeration to say that the group is "united by (neuro)diversity"—diversity is just about the only thing that unites this bunch of "dreamers and fighters." And yet it emerges that diversity brings many benefits both to researchers and to their research.

Notes

1. Following Nick Walker, we define "neurodivergent" as "having a mind that functions in ways which diverge significantly from the dominant societal standards of 'normal.'" A neurodiverse group includes people who "differ substantially from [each other], in terms of their neurocognitive functioning." As such, a neurodiverse group can include both neurotypical and neurodivergent people (Walker, 2021, pp. 33–46, quotations on pp. 38, 42).
2. Some people who identify with other neurodivergences than autism have pointed out that in some discussions neurodivergence seems to be equated with autism. That is not the intention here. The only reason the focus of our work, and hence this article, is on autism is because that is the focus of the Centre for Autism and Theology. At the same time, the Centre welcomes people who identify with other neurodivergences, which is why these are mentioned here too.
3. https://www.abdn.ac.uk/sdhp/centre-for-the-study-of-autism-and-christian-community-1725.php#panel2095, last accessed on April 21st 2023.
4. Existing literature on this topic was found to relate only to undergraduate experience. For example, we discussed an article by Van Hees et al. (2015). We also reviewed the following two websites providing toolkits and resources: https://imageautism.com; https://www.autism-uni.org.
5. A recent article on autistic researchers in academia foregrounds the voices of autistic academics, but this is not based on postgraduate researchers (Jones, 2023).
6. Insofar as known—people are never asked to reveal anything about their identity in this group that they do not want to share. It should be noted that a relatively high percentage of neurodivergent people identifies as other than cisgender. Similarly, we have never asked group members about their sexual orientation.

Disclosure statement

No potential conflict of interest was reported by the author(s).

References

Cameron, H., Bhatti, D., Duce, C., Sweeney, J., & Watkins, C. (2010). *Talking about god in practice: Theological action research and practical theology*. SCM Press.
Cook, J., Hull, L., Crane, L., & Mandy, W. (2021). Camouflaging in autism: A systematic review. *Clinical Psychology Review, 89*, 102080. https://doi.org/10.1016/j.cpr.2021.102080

Jones, S. C. (2023). Advice for autistic people considering a career in academia. *Autism: The International Journal of Research and Practice, 27*(7), 2187–2192. https://doi.org/10.1177/13623613231161882

Kember, D., Ha, T.-S., Lam, B.-H., Lee, A., Ng, S., Yan, L., & Yum, J. C. K. (1997). The diverse role of the critical friend in supporting educational action research projects. *Educational Action Research, 5*(3), 463–481. https://doi.org/10.1080/09650799700200036

Macaskill, G. (2019). *Autism and the church: Bible, theology, and community.* Baylor University Press.

Miller, D., Rees, J., & Pearson, A. (2021). "Masking is life": Experiences of masking in autistic and nonautistic adults. *Autism in Adulthood: Challenges and Management, 3*(4), 330–338. https://doi.org/10.1089/aut.2020.0083

Milton, D. E. M. (2012). On the ontological status of autism: The 'double empathy problem'. *Disability & Society, 27*(6), 883–887. https://doi.org/10.1080/09687599.2012.710008

Norrelgen, F., Fernell, E., Eriksson, M., Hedvall, Å., Persson, C., Sjölin, M., Gillberg, C., & Kjellmer, L. (2015). Children with autism spectrum disorders who do not develop phrase speech in the preschool years. *Autism, 19*(8), 934–943. https://doi.org/10.1177/1362361314556782

Rapley, S. (2021). *Autistic thinking in the life of the church.* SCM Press.

Russell, G., Mandy, W., Elliott, D., White, R., Pittwood, T., & Ford, T. (2019). Selection bias on intellectual ability in autism research: A cross-sectional review and meta-analysis. *Molecular Autism, 10*(1), 9. https://doi.org/10.1186/s13229-019-0260-x

Sedgewick, F., Hull, L., & Ellis, H. (2022). *Autism and masking: How and why people do it, and the impact it can have.* Jessica Kingsley Publishers.

Van Hees, V., Moyson, T., & Roeyers, H. (2015). Higher education experiences of students with autism spectrum disorder: Challenges, benefits and support needs. *Journal of Autism and Developmental Disorders, 45*(6), 1673–1688. https://doi.org/10.1007/s10803-014-2324-2

Van Ommen, A. L. (2023). *Autism and worship: A liturgical theology.* Baylor University Press.

Waldock, K. E. (2023). The impossible subject: Belonging as a neurodivergent in congregations. *Journal of Disability & Religion,* 1–16. https://doi.org/10.1080/23312521.2023.2249452

Waldock, K. E., & Keates, N. (2022). Autistic voices in autistic research: Towards active citizenship in autism research. In S. Ryan & D. Milton (Eds.), *The Routledge international handbook of critical autism studies* (pp. 288–302). Routledge.

Walker, N. (2021). *Neuroqueer heresies: Notes on the neurodiversity paradigm, autistic empowerment, and postnormal possibilities.* Autonomous Press.

"Misfitting" and Friendship in the Virtuous Life: Neurodiversity and Moral Formation

Elizabeth Agnew Cochran

ABSTRACT

The self-reported experiences of autistic individuals invite ways of thinking about moral character and moral formation that challenge Christians to rethink a number of traditional claims regarding the virtues. This paper argues that attention to autism requires rethinking accounts of growth in virtue that depend on normative views of social interactions such as friendship. Drawing on scholarship in disability studies and testimony from autistic participants in an IRB-supported research study, I contend that the phenomenon of "misfitting" put forth in the work of Rosemarie Garland-Thomson (2011) plays a constructive and essential role in shaping virtuous character.

Introduction

As recently as the beginning of the twenty-first century, it was commonplace for psychologists and philosophers to associate autism with limited moral capacities. Autistic individuals were characterized as having a significantly diminished capacity for empathy, a term that psychologists associated with a cognitive ability to assume the perspective of others, known as "theory of mind."[1] Presumptions about this autistic deficit in empathy led scientists likewise to overlook autistic persons' existence as complex moral beings, attributing to them only a very rudimentary sort of moral agency and a limited kind of moral responsibility.[2] The neurodiversity movement has contributed to a shift in the past fifteen years such that many scholars in psychology, anthropology, and a number of social sciences increasingly recognize that autistic people exercise empathy (particularly when understood as emotional concern for others' well-being) in ways that were previously overlooked due to the biases of researchers and the limitations of theoretical frameworks that sought to measure empathy. These developing understandings of the ways in which autistic individuals exercise empathy laid the groundwork for a new recognition that autistic individuals function as moral agents, that they both pursue and value particular moral qualities, and that they are capable of exercising and embodying virtues.[3]

The language of virtue is important to this understanding of autistic people as capable of being part of the moral community, not simply as arbitrary rule-followers but as active and reflective participants. Virtues are stable character traits that are widely held to be morally good and that promote *eudaimonia*, the flourishing that is the *telos* or end of human beings (Annas 2011). Ascribing virtues to someone is a way of saying that moral commitments are embodied in particular character traits that are central to who we are, as people, and that affect all dimensions of our lives. Christians have historically drawn on and transformed philosophical accounts of the virtues that were first articulated in thinkers such as Aristotle and the Stoics. Contemporary Christian virtue ethicists take a number of different approaches to the virtues (Herdt 2015), but we can broadly say that the Christian tradition understands the virtues as means through which human beings are formed in Christ's character and brought into deeper relation with God as part of being shaped into the people God has called us to be. Thomas Aquinas identifies faith, hope, and love as the theological virtues, which particularly guide us toward our *telos* or end of friendship with God. Christian theology generally conceives the incarnate Jesus Christ as an exemplar of the virtues, embodying character traits that are constitutive of the good life and a central means through which human beings relate to our Creator. A recognition of Jesus Christ as an exemplar of the virtues leads to identifying certain character traits exemplified by Christ as virtues. These qualities include humility (Cochran 2011) and love, particularly a form of love for God and neighbor that both emulates and participates in God's universal love (Jackson 2003, Clark 2014, Nothwehr 2016).

A recognition of autistic individuals as capable of pursuing the virtues challenges Christians to rethink traditional accounts of both what a virtuous life looks like and how a person is formed in it. Virtue ethicists put forth a number of claims that associate the virtues with capacities to navigate social relations, an approach that risks building on and reinscribing a normative understanding of what constitutes virtuous and vicious social interactions. For example, Nancy Snow (2010) conceives the virtues as forms of "social intelligence" through which an agent navigates social structures and interactions in a manner informed by morally good motivations (86). It is worth noting that Snow indirectly acknowledges that this definition excludes autistic persons from having the capacity to exercise virtue. She presents Christopher, the autistic protagonist of Mark Haddon's novel and play *The Curious Incident of the Dog in the Nighttime* as an example of someone who does not show social intelligence, describing autism as a "social impairment" that is "permanent," in part because "the ability to interpret facial expressions is an essential and basic component of both social competence and social intelligence" (p. 78). The virtues are also traditionally connected to social interactions in considerations of "practical rationality," which functions, particularly in Aristotelian and Thomistic moral theory, as a core virtue that guides all other virtues and enables a moral agent to exercise these virtues in everyday life. David Cloutier and Anthony Ahrens (2020) argue that a central part of practical rationality is the ability correctly to appraise the situations in which we find ourselves and to discern what sorts of actions are appropriate to these situations (p. 340). In different ways, such accounts of the virtues understand good character traits and good actions in a manner shaped by neurotypical views of what it means to navigate social relationships appropriately and effectively. The neurodiversity movement points toward the limitations of accounts that have actively excluded autistic perspectives for conceiving the good life[4] in a manner attentive to the nature and ends of humanity as a whole and calls for ways of thinking about virtues and moral formation that more adequately account for neurological variation in the human species.

In addition to understanding the virtues themselves in a manner that prioritizes navigating social relations effectively, both philosophical and theological accounts of the virtues understand moral formation as largely occurring through social relationships. Virtue ethicists recognize a number of ways in which human beings learn to be moral in relation with others: we learn through observing and emulating moral exemplars (Zagzebski 2017), through participating in communities of shared deliberation (MacIntyre 2016), through taking part in friendship with others (Cates 1996, Hauerwas & Pinches 1997, Brewer 2005, Kristjansson 2020). Certainly friendship and good relationships with others are important to humans' well-being and flourishing. Human beings are social, and connections to others are a good to be celebrated. Hans Reinders (2008) is not wrong to contend that friendship is the central good for human beings (pp. 6-8, pp. 162-163). Likewise, Neely Myers (2016) makes a compelling case that "peopled opportunities" are important to flourishing, and that such opportunities for meaningful relationships of mutual accountability provide settings in which human beings are formed in good character by practicing whom we want to be (p. 438). But while friendship is a genuine good for human beings, there are variations in circumstances that make it more available and more easy to cultivate in some contexts than others. I will suggest below that a consideration of neurodiversity invites us to think more carefully about how experiences of feeling out of sync with one's community can benefit our growth in virtue.

This essay proposes one way that neurodiversity can enrich current understandings of moral formation, drawing both on scholarship from disability studies and testimony from participants in an IRB-supported research study[5] that involved qualitative analysis of 45-60 min interviews with 18 autistic teenagers and adults and 12 parents of autistic persons. Attention to neurodiversity offers insight into the constructive and necessary role the phenomenon of "misfitting," articulated in the work of Rosemarie Garland-Thomson (2011), plays in shaping virtuous character. I offer two related claims: first, inattention to the relational and contextual phenomena of "fitting" and "misfitting" contributes to the failure of many of us—Christian theologians, scholars in other fields, clergy, and churches— to recognize virtues at work in autistic lives. This tendency, and its negative impact on our assessments of autistic virtue, is demonstrated through reflecting on the "double empathy problem" put forth by Damian Milton (2012). Second, attention to "misfitting" provides a way of thinking about the cultivation and achievement of the virtues that is less dependent on certain social advantages than some traditional models of moral formation uphold. Drawing on Garland-Thomson, Shane Clifton (2018) affirms that "misfitting has the potential for generative power; misfits can be agents of social transformation" (p. 156). The experience of misfitting can likewise play a central role in developing a virtuous character.

Misfitting and the "double empathy problem"

One of the most important and influential critiques of the association of autism with a deficit in empathy calls attention to the relational contexts in which empathy is felt, practiced, and interpreted, contexts that challenge a model that associates autism with an absence of a capacity that is present in most people. Damian Milton (2012) coins the term the "double empathy problem" to explain precisely how deficit-based views of autism, particularly those concluding that autistic persons lack empathy based on psychological studies, emerge from scientists' misinterpreted characterizations of social interactions. The "double empathy problem" signals that interactive challenges between any two parties, including a nonautistic researcher and an autistic participant in a research study, are failures of "reciprocity and mutuality" that can be attributed to both parties and to the interaction itself. Experiments that lead to conclusions that people with autism lack empathy do not actually demonstrate that people with autism lack moral capacities, but instead that when non-autistic researchers observe their behaviors, these researchers misinterpret the behaviors' meanings. The "problem" Milton identifies is thus not a deficit in empathy located in an autistic person, but an interpretive limitation affecting interactions between autistic and nonautistic people. Just as autistic people often lack insight into neurotypical behavioral norms and expectations, so do neurotypical people often lack insight into autistic culture and modes of being.

Milton's compelling rejection of a deficit-based account of autism as an absence of empathy complements Garland-Thomson's 2011 account of "misfitting" as a model for understanding disability. Garland-Thomson makes use of the concept of "misfit" to reflect on "the lived identity and experience of disability as it is situated in place and time" (p. 591). The term "misfit" offers a way of understanding disability as a relational phenomenon: the terms "fit" and "misfit" navigate the relation between "body and world," describing an encounter between a person and their environment and noting the ways that this relation does or does not align. As terms that describe a relation, rather than the beings in that relation, "fitting" and "misfitting" can change and shift as persons navigate different contexts (pp. 592-593). Moreover, these concepts are not descriptive simply of disabilities in the abstract, but of the lived experience of disability as specific individuals and contexts navigate it. Garland-Thomson affirms that the concept of fitness stresses the ways that "disability" functions as a relational concept but simultaneously acknowledges the reality of disability's effects on embodied human existence. She emphasizes the concrete reality of misfitting, explaining that misfitting is a category that resists a "theoretical generic disabled body" and allows for particular "varying lived embodiments" (p. 592).

Just as Milton's argument that the "double empathy problem" rejects the idea that this "problem" is located in autistic individuals, one of Garland-Thomson's key claims is that the concept of misfitting resists the idea that disability is a deficit located in a disabled person. She affirms that the "problem" of misfitting is something that "inheres not in either of the two things" that encounter each other, but in the "discrepancy between body and world, between that which is expected and that which is" (p. 593). In the decade following Milton's publication, several studies in psychology have shared this recognition that failures in communication and mutual understanding are common between autistic and non-autistic persons. These studies suggest that neurotypical people have trouble understanding the emotions and expressions of autistic people (Sheppard et al. 2016, Edey et al. 2016), that autistic people have trouble understanding the emotions and expressions of neurotypical people (Cassidy et al. 2014), and that autistic people may more easily understand the expressions and emotions of other autistic people (Komeda et al., 2015). But even as such studies suggest the prevalence of misfitting and the failure of non-autistic researchers to understand the communication and intentions of autistic research participants, Milton importantly emphasizes that autistic people are at greater risk of being harmed by flawed conclusions researchers draw from observations of their behavior. As Milton explains, autistic people are "othered" and characterized in terms that are pathologized and damaging when they fail to meet the expectations of researchers. When researchers in positions of power develop studies of particular populations and draw conclusions about the character of those populations, they risk causing serious harm by the conclusions they draw.

Contemporary Christian theologians and pastors should be attentive to the concept of misfitting and the double empathy problem, and reflect on the ways that overlooking these phenomena has contributed to personal and institutional biases and presumptions about the moral capacities of autistic persons. My research study attempted to recognize the risk of falling prey to the double empathy problem by employing an interview format, which gave epistemic priority to first person narrative testimony of autistic individuals.[6] I also attempted to structure these conversations and to code the interviews in a manner that avoided interpreting our dialogue through the lens of overly narrow and rigid philosophical and theological accounts of the virtues, though it is inevitable that some measure of unconscious bias shapes the interpretive lens of all researchers. The studies I noted in the preceding paragraph likewise suggest awareness that researchers need to guard against the double empathy problem in the design and execution of their studies. But despite this increased awareness of the double empathy problem in certain sciences, the idea that autistic people lack a theory of mind continues to have wide influence. Belek and Stasch (2019) suggests that research on autism reflects two different "analytic poles" with an "epistemic gap." Fields such as anthropology tend to think of autism as a "socio-political category," and fields such as psychology tend to think of autism as a "neurodevelopmental disorder." In the latter sorts of fields, scholarship associating autism with various specific deficits, such as a deficit in theory of mind or executive functioning skills, remains common. For example, Livingston et al. (2019) and Rosello et al. (2020) both consider why certain autistic people are able to demonstrate social skills despite lacking a theory of mind; Rosello et al. begin their study by affirming that "literature showing that individuals with ASD display deficits in ToM is extensive and robust." A brief consideration of Milton and Garland-Thomson urges Christians to be cautious about taking such accounts of autism at face value, especially insofar as these accounts reiterate a view of autism as characterized primarily by deficits located in the autistic person. Reconceiving the "problem" of autism in terms of the fit between person and environment is an important step in reexamining how overly narrow views of the good life neglect neurologically diverse ways of understanding the character of the good life in human beings.

Misfitting and formation in the virtues

As noted above, traditional views of virtue uphold friendship and social relations as central means through which human beings learn to become virtuous. But the social contexts into which human beings are born vary widely, such that some people have more natural access to resources and supports than others. Some of the means through which human beings are formed socially in the virtues depend partly on factors outside our control: for example, family, teachers, and coaches who serve as good and supportive exemplars, churches that offer effective supports and a safe space in which to learn and grow, and external resources that facilitate our participation in formative practices and communities.[7] Neurodiversity can also affect the processes through which people engage in social relationships; Jacobs and Richardson (2022) offer qualitative examples suggesting that friendship can be difficult for neurodivergent people. A consideration of neurodiversity broadens our understanding of the contexts in which humans are formed in the virtues to recognize that experiences of being out of sync with one's community can benefit our growth in the virtues. The idea that misfitting can be part of moral formation helpfully expands how Christians think about the processes through which human beings acquire good character.

Autism offers one distinctive way of thinking about precisely what misfitting may look like. On one hand, autism is characterized by a sense of oneself as embodying a distinct "form of life" (as Chapman 2019 puts it, drawing on Wittgenstein), that can make autistic persons feel like aliens in neurotypical society. Yet paradoxically, autism is simultaneously characterized by a profound sense of connection between oneself and the world. Drawing on examples from my research, I will argue below that autistic persons are able to embody a virtuous love of neighbor—a sense of compassion and concern for justice—that emerges from this sense of self as deeply connected to the world, while sometimes simultaneously experiencing strained relationships with immediate family and friends, due in part to differences in communication introduced above. This particular form of autistic misfitting, experiencing oneself as an alien and simultaneously deeply connected to the world, gives rise to an account of virtue that can emerge even as one navigates an uneasy relationship with one's formative communities.

Jim Sinclair's 1993 talk "Don't Mourn for Us," a text that played a pivotal role in establishing the neurodiversity movement,[8] uses the trope of "aliens" to describe the mode of misfitting characteristic of autistic persons' experiences in a society structured around neurotypical norms and expectations. Addressed to parents of autistic children, Sinclair's talk challenges parents to understand autism not as a disease to be lamented, but a distinctive "way of being." This way of being in the world is different from how nonautistic persons, including nonautistic parents, experience the world. Sinclair explains that autistic children and their parents do not communicate through a "shared system, a shared understanding of signals and meanings." Autistic people, Sinclair explains, are "'foreigners' in any society" who successfully engage the society around them only by "operating in alien territory, making contact with alien beings." Sinclair concludes his talk by returning to the argument that autistic children inhabit the world as aliens. An autistic child is "an alien child…a child, stranded in an alien world, without parents of its own kind to care for it." Autistic children are alien children, misfits who do not inhabit the world the same way nonautistic persons do.

At the same time, other accounts of autism suggest that this "alien" way of being in the world is characterized by a profound sense of connection with the world that gives rise to a capacity for a particularly deep empathy. Neuroscientists Kamila Markram and Henry Markram (2007, 2010) put forth the "intense world theory" as a way of describing the overwhelming nature of autistic persons' reception of sensory and emotional input in the world. Autistic persons, they explain, process the world in such intensified ways that they become overwhelmed by emotions and appear to withdraw. The pain and aversion Markram and Markram connect to intense experiences of the world is corroborated by participants in my research study, a number of whom spoke of feeling things too much or too deeply, and of being so hyper-aware of the sensory world that they found it overwhelming. For example, Tom, an autistic man in his 50s, says that his "antennae" are up and deeply, at times painfully, aware of others' emotions and of sensory input. Marcus, an autistic man in his 40s, similarly describes his emotions as intense. He explains that his emotions are at odds with neurotypical expectations both in the degree of their intensity and in the objects or circumstances that generate them: "what I always tell people is, my emotions are on 25. If the dial goes 1 to 10, my emotions are at 25. And I do not generally feel emotionally connected to the things that a neurotypical person would expect me to feel emotionally connected to."

But while the challenges associated with such an intense experience of the world should not be overlooked, feelings of deep connection between oneself and the world are not always or necessarily painful. Moreover, these feelings ground a way of understanding oneself in relation to the world that gives rise to a virtuous compassion rooted in a deep empathy. Karla McLaren (2013), for example, identifies autistic people are "hyper-empaths." Autistic psychologist Nick Walker cites McLaren and "recent findings in neuroscience" in an argument against the conclusions of Frith and Baron-Cohen about autistic capacities for empathy.[9] This sense of deep empathy is fostered by a more intellectualized way of understanding oneself as closely related to the rest of the world, a self-understanding that complements the emotional and sensory bombardment described in Markram and Markram and that serves as a rational mechanism through which autistic individuals can begin to make sense of this bombardment and to see it, at least partially, as a positive thing. Elizabeth Fein (2020) associates autism with a "permeable" sense of self, a sense that the surrounding environment is an extension of one's own identity. Drawing on Charles Taylor's association of a "buffered" self—a clear boundary between self and other—with modernity, she suggests that people on the spectrum tend to have an "experience of … the lived self-in-the-world," that is "more porous than is the norm for their late modern cultural milieu" (2020, p. 237). She advocates understanding autism itself as a "mode of engagement" with the world that involves a "deep existential vulnerability" (2018, p. 130) and contends that the category of autism should be expanded to include the cultural "content" with which autistic people interact (2018, p. 133).

Importantly, for Fein, this sense of oneself as closely related to one's environment is not a fantasy invented by the autistic brain. Instead, it reflects insight into a genuine connection that exists between human brains and the surrounding world. Fein contends that it is misleading to think of human brain activity, autistic or otherwise, in isolation from culture. "Human cognition is inextricable from culture, and … the kind of cognitive processes that get labeled 'autistic,' rather than being exceptions to this rule, are instead exemplars of it" (2020, p. 33). Fein explains that this interplay between individual brain and environment is at work in the process of conducting a neuropsychological evaluation for autism, which involves observing and evaluating how autistic person interacts with his or her environment (2020, p. 64). While most scientific literature erroneously works to "locate the origins of what manifests as autism exclusively within the individual minds of those diagnosed" (2020, p. 33), Fein invites us to think of the terms at play in this process of understanding precisely what constitutes autism—such as "executive function" and "theory of mind"—not as capacities located in an individual brain, but capacities that are constituted by an interaction of person with the person's social world (2020, p. 33). In making this argument, Fein contends not simply that we should resist thinking of autism as in some sense located within individual brains, but that we should rethink the meaning of a number of human activities that are not uniquely associated with autism. When we treat autism as a pathology, she argues, we reinforce a normative "impossible ideal of a pure individual self, uncorrupted by materials of human making" and reject accounts of human being that see human selves and relations as partly constituted by culture and its associated products, such as forms of technology, and by the natural world (2018, p. 149).

Autism is thus a way of being in the world that "misfits" from social structures framed by neurotypical norms in two ways. Autistic experience of neurotypical society can be framed as "alien" encounters, and at the same time, autistic experience of the surrounding environment is so "intense" that the autistic sense of self expands to include a deep sense of connection with one's environment. Both of these features of autistic misfitting encourage reflection on how an autistic way of inhabiting the world—and particularly of "misfitting" as they navigate life in communities that are centered around neurotypical norms and expectations—can be morally formative. Garland-Thomson affirms that the concept of misfitting provides disabled subjects with agency associated with the particular strengths and capacities that come from not fitting in. These strengths include "adaptability, resourcefulness, and subjugated knowledge" (2011, p. 592). Not only is misfitting formative for misfits themselves, it is also formative for those who observe them. The act of misfitting provides a witness to those who "fit" at a given moment, teaching them to be more attentive to their circumstances and to the contingency of "fitting" into one's environment. In contrast to the mundane experience of fitting, which is "a comfortable and unremarkable majority experience of material ano-nymity," misfitting is a reminder of the "relational component and the fragility of fitting" (2011, p. 597). Fitting is comfortable, but it also bears a potential "cost" in the form of "complacency about social justice and a desensitizing the material experience" (2011, p. 597). Misfitting challenges those who are fitting to be attentive to the complexity and fragility of human life.

But not only do misfits teach the "fit" persons who observe them, they themselves also learn and grow through the process of misfitting, so that misfitting becomes a mode through which one has potential to be formed in the virtues. Garland-Thomson affirms that misfitting establishes a mate-rial and particular identity for individual disabled persons. She maintains that disabled persons' "individual and collective experience of misfitting" can provide a starting point for a self-understanding that is empowering and "liberatory," for a sense of identity that provides a vantage point for unique forms of engaging and responding to the world (2011, p. 601). In misfitting, dissonance with one's community becomes a source for agency and empowerment.

The form of human misfitting that autism illuminates has the potential to be morally formative by creating a sense of one's self and one's rela-tionship to the world that motivates a commitment to justice and com-passion, two virtues that are associated with a universal concern for the well being of others. Studies have suggested that both of these virtues may be particularly present in many autistic persons (Sterponi 2004, Dempsey et al. 2020). Likewise, the story of Marcus, one participant in my research study, embodies this commitment and illustrates how this profound sense of other-regard can emerge even while misfitting. Marcus sees himself as subject to a "moral imperative" that "drives" him and "wakes [him] up every morning." "I am driven, to the point of compulsion, about doing what's right. Doing good, doing right." This consuming desire to promote the good, as Marcus understands it, is consistent with a virtuous compassion that is universally directed toward all humans. When I asked Marcus to explain how he understands moral goodness, he defined it in terms of an inclusive love and kindness: "For me, good is what makes the world better. For me, it all comes down to doing the most loving and kind thing possible. I am very much driven by, how do we make the world a place where everybody can be okay, where it can be inclusive and loving for everyone?" He explains that he has worked for over twenty years in social services and has strong desires to help people and promote the good, both in the sense of supporting the persons he encounters and in the sense of rethinking systems to ameliorate injustice: "I'm not kidding you when I tell you that I have a plan to end poverty in America. Like, I'm not joking! That's the way I think."

Marcus describes longstanding efforts to pursue and embody compassion and justice. At the same time, his experience of these virtues is coupled with lifelong experiences of misfitting. The "moral imperative" that he describes as driving him emerges from his way of inhabiting the world, which involves a profound sense of feeling connected to the world as a whole while also feeling "alien," particularly in interactions with his family of origin. Marcus does not articulate a sense of connection to the world or environment, as some other participants in my study did, but he articulates a sense of moral responsibility toward the world: "I have forever been just extremely driven toward helping people, and doing the right thing and being a help to the world. I have this intense desire to do something that matters." Yet this sense of connection and responsibility stands alongside lifelong experiences of misfitting. Though Marcus was diagnosed as an adult, he explains that a sense of feeling "different" marked his childhood: "I have always known that I was a little different. My entire life I've been hearing that... People would say things like 'Marcus's just different.'" Likewise, despite his commitments to justice and love, Marcus indicates that he struggles in many of his closest interpersonal relationships: "I would say over the last ten years ...I was noticing strains in all of my closest relationships, that all had the same sort of pattern." He recounts stories of inadvertently hurting the feelings of a family member, making a different family member angry by pressing them to rethink some of their personal habits, and making his partner frustrated when he did not hold clients accountable for paying for his professional counseling services. Indeed, reflecting on these strained relationships was one factor that led Marcus to explore the possibility that he might be autistic and to undergo assessments that led to his diagnosis. Marcus says that his diagnosis has not been helpful in his relationships with his family of origin, but it has been helpful for him, giving him tools to make sense of how "someone of my knowledge and skill set" could "have this many social problems." Marcus's story raises questions about the relation of virtuous, universal love to love for family and friends that are outside the scope of this essay. For now, it is important to note that Marcus's experiences of autism are associated with a lifelong sense of feeling "different" and of having strained relationships with family as a result. But his story also shows how virtue can emerge in the midst of a life characterized by misfitting, and potentially even through misfitting.

Marcus's testimony does not explicitly explore how misfitting can directly lead to virtue, but other participants in my study more directly explain how their advocacy for others is rooted in a sense of empathy or compassion acquired, in part, through their own misfitting. The experience of misfitting provided these participants with a vantage point from which to recognize the particular needs of individuals at risk for being marginalized. Adam, a 20 year old nonspeaking autistic individual, and Katherine, an autistic woman in her 50s, both express a strong commitment to justice on behalf of other autistics who are nonspeaking, and suggest that this commitment was formed in them through earlier experiences of being able to communicate less consistently with neurotypicals. Adam, a 20-year-old autistic man, completed an interview with me by communicating through spelling words with a laminated alphabet board. He had learned to communicate through this practice approximately six months prior to our interview. He expressed great joy in having learned to communicate in this way, affirming that this mode of communication allows him to take part in social interactions in a way that he never could before: "I am so happy now that I can communicate. I can participate in social things. I am loving that." Having only recently learned how to communicate in a way that could be understood by his neurotypical family, Adam feels particular sympathy for those who are nonspeaking: "it was awful when I did not have a voice." Yet he feels that the experience of autism, and especially of having been nonspeaking for a number of years, "enriched" his life through equipping him with a unique capacity for sympathy. He explains that he can be "sympathetic with lots of kinds of people… I have suffered, so I know what it feels like to be excluded." I asked if he feels like he can perceive or sense the emotions of others who are excluded in groups, and he affirmed, "Yes, I can feel their pain. I am so happy you asked, because a lot of people don't know that autistics are really tuned in." Adam went on to explain that he "want[s] to help" those who do not have a voice, and suggested that he, as someone whose life had been "unlocked" by learning to spell, felt particularly tuned in to the experience of being nonspeaking. The experience of misfitting helped him feel particularly equipped to express justice and compassion toward others.

Katherine articulated a similar sense of responsibility to speak on behalf of less verbal autistic individuals. Katherine teaches yoga to other autistic individuals, and says that in the course of interacting with others with varying verbal abilities, she has come to feel particular empathy for the challenges of being misinterpreted. The nonspeaking are at risk for having others put "words in their mouths" and say "This is how they feel," but, Katherine explains, "Just because they're nonverbal doesn't mean—like, 'We don't need your interpretation, because that's not how it's actually happening.'" Nonspeaking autistic people, Katherine affirms, can be "brilliant," but often feel "trapped." When I asked her about moral qualities that she sees as important in her own life, Katherine immediately communicated a strong sense of responsibility for using her experience of being autistic to speak on behalf of autistic individuals who struggle to communicate as effectively with neurotypical peers: "It's that, being able to speak up, speaking for those who can't speak, or for those who have been silenced and want to speak. It's from a victim's standpoint. It's that, you have a duty. And, you will never be subject to that again. So you do everything you can do, if you can do it. And you try to find ways—new ways, if you can't do it this way, then you try to find a new way. Or you engage others who can maybe help. But it's not okay to have knowledge about something that does not work, that harms someone, and not change it. If you can." Adam and Katherine illustrate how their own experiences of misfitting—being out of sync with society's expectations and communication systems—have given them an intellectual perspective on the needs of others and generated an emotional sympathy for others that have helped to form their commitments to justice and compassion.

Conclusion

Human beings are naturally inclined toward relations with others, and these relationships with others are a characteristically human good that partly constitute our flourishing. But ethicists have tended to advance overly narrow conceptions of the virtues and the process through which we are formed in them that overlook the variety of experiences human beings have within particular communities. This tendency and its problematic effects can be found in reflecting on the double empathy problem and the ways in which nonautistic researchers have historically tended to view autistic individuals as having limited moral capacities. A more expansive view of moral formation recognizes that there are a number of circumstances in which people might struggle to participate in communities that have the potential to be a source of meaningful relationships that help us grow in virtue, but that this need not make virtue inaccessible to them.

The phenomenon of misfitting, particularly as it can at times play out in the experience of autistic individuals, calls attention to the ways that a sense of being an outsider or alien can contribute positively to moral growth. A sense of disconnect between oneself and one's community need not be at odds with a profound sense of kinship with the human species and the broader world, and this dual experience of misfitting and kinship can be fruitful for cultivating a sense of compassion and a concern for justice. Likewise, misfitting can provide an intellectual lens through which one is able to evaluate social structures with particular attunement to the need of those at risk for marginalization, and to feel a sense of sympathy that begins the process of formation in virtue.

The experiences of participants in my study illustrate that misfitting can be a mechanism through which neurodivergent individuals are formed in the virtues. But these experiences also press us to recognize that misfitting can offer a sense of perspective about the needs of others and the moral limitations of the communities we inhabit that helps both autistic and nonautistic persons be more compassionate and just than we might be when unquestioningly enmeshed in our communities. Just as prophets effectively speak to the needs of their institutions and communities partly thorugh occupying a space that is not a neat "fit" with these institutions, so can misfits more generally grow in compassion and justice through embracing the intellectual and emotional perspectives offered to them through the act of misfitting.

Notes

1. Premack and Woodruff (1978) first used this term to describe a cognitive ability to infer the perspective of others. Simon Baron-Cohen, Alan Leslie, and Uta Frith (1985) assessed theory of mind in autistic children on the basis of a false-belief task in a laboratory setting, and concluded that the capacity for theory of mind in autistic children is diminished. This study had a significant influence on subsequent research. Baron-Cohen's subsequent work turned explicitly to empathy, demonstrating a presumption that empathy builds on and requires a capacity to interpret other people's mental states. He developed a psychological questionnaire called the Empathy Quotient (EQ), designed to measure empathy in adults with IQs in the normal range. In an early publication communicating results of a study that made use of this questionnaire, Baron-Cohen and Wheelwright (2004) argued that autism is associated not simply with a diminished theory of mind, but more explicitly with a deficit in empathy.
2. See, for example, Barnbaum, 2008, Shoemaker, 2015.
3. See, for example, Dempsey et al., 2020.
4. John Swinton (2012) contends that autistic voices have historically been excluded from Christian accounts of love in particular.
5. This research study, "Friendship, Spirituality, and Autistic Well-Being," is conducted at Duquesne University and was initially approved by Duquesne University's Institutional Review Board on May 1, 2021. The IRB number is 2021/02/7.

6. Barnes (2016), drawing on the work of Miranda Fricker, explains that "testimonial injustice," dismissing the testimony and experience of disabled persons, is a form of epistemic injustice. In giving narrative testimony pride of place, my study attempts to counter this injustice.
7. A philosophical debate about the "moral luck" offers tools for thinking further about the role these situational and contextual factors play in moral formation, and the degree to which it is fair to hold moral agents responsible for factors outside our control. See, for example, Williams & Nagel 1976, Zimmerman 2015.
8. For more on this history, see Pripas-Kapit 2020.
9. Walker speaks positively of McLaren's work in a 2015 interview included in Norm Kunc's *Conversations That Matter* series. Video of this interview can be found on https://neuroqueer.com/autism-empathy-and-theory-of-mind/ (accessed December 10, 2021).

Acknowledgments

The research and writing of this essay were supported by Collaborations in Christian Theological Anthropology, a project affiliated with Villanova University and the John Templeton Foundation, and New Visions in Theological Anthropology, a project affiliated with St. Andrew's University and the John Templeton Foundation. I am grateful to colleagues from both projects who read and provided feedback on versions of these arguments, and particularly to John Bowlin and Elizabeth Fein.

Disclosure statement

No potential conflict of interest was reported by the author.

Funding

John Templeton Foundation

References

Annas, J. (2011). *Intelligent virtue*. Oxford University Press.
Barnbaum, D. (2008). *The ethics of autism: Among them, but not of them*. Indiana University Press.
Barnes, E. (2016). *The minority body: A theory of disability*. Oxford University Press.
Baron-Cohen, S., Leslie, A., & Frith, U. (1985). Does the autistic child have a 'theory of mind? *Cognition, 21*(1), 37–46. https://doi.org/10.1016/0010-0277(85)90022-8
Baron-Cohen, S., & Wheelwright, S. (2004). The empathy quotient: An investigation of adults with apserger syndrome or high functioning autism, and normal sex differences. *Journal of Autism and Developmental Disorders, 34*(2), 163–175. https://doi.org/10.1023/b:Jadd.0000022607.19833.00
Belek, B. (2019) 2023. Autism. *The Open Encyclopedia of Anthropology*, edited by Felix Stein. Fascimile of tthe first edition in *Cambridge Encyclopedia of Anthropology*. Online: https://doi.org/10.29164/19aut
Brewer, T. (2005). Virtues we can share: Friendship and Aristotelian ethical theory. *Ethics, 115*(4), 721–758. https://doi.org/10.1086/430489

Cassidy, S., Ropar, D., Mitchell, P., & Chapman, P. (2014). Can adults with autism spectrum disorder infer what happened to someone from their emotional response? *Autism Research : official Journal of the International Society for Autism Research*, 7(1), 112–123. https://doi.org/10.1002/aur.1351

Cates, D. (1996). *Choosing to feel: Virtue, friendship, and compassion for friends.* University of Notre Dame Press.

Chapman, R. (2019). Autism as a form of life: Wittgenstein and the psychological coherence of autism. *Metaphilosophy*, 50(4), 421–440. https://doi.org/10.1111/meta.12366

Clark, P. M. (2014). The case for the exemplarist approach to virtue in catholic moral theology. *Journal of Moral Theology*, 3(1), 54–82.

Clifton, S. (2018). *Crippled grace: Disability, virtue ethics, and the good life.* Baylor University Press.

Cloutier, D., & Ahrens, A. H. (2020). Catholic moral theology and the virtues: Integrating psychology in models of moral agency. *Theological Studies*, 81(2), 326–347. https://doi.org/10.1177/0040563920928563

Dempsey, E., Moore, C., Richard, A. E., & Smith, I. M. (2020). Moral foundations theory in autism spectrum disorder: A qualitative investigation. *Autism: The International Journal of Research and Practice*, 24(8), 2202–2212. https://doi.org/10.1177/1362361320939331

Edey, R., Cook, J., Brewer, R., Johnson, M., Bird, G., & Press, C. (2016). Interaction takes two: Typical adults exhibit mind-blindness towards those with autism spectrum disorder. *Journal of Abnormal Psychology*, 125(7), 879–885. https://doi.org/10.1037/abn0000199

Fein, E. (2018). Autism as a mode of engagement. In E. Fein & C. Rios (Eds.), *Autism in translation: An intercultural conversation on autism spectrum conditions* (pp. 129–154). Palgrave Macmillan.

Fein, E. (2020). *Living on the spectrum: Autism and youth in community.* New York University Press.

Garland-Thomson, R. (2011). Misfits: A feminist materialist disability concept. *Hypatia*, 26(3), 591–609. https://doi.org/10.1111/j.1527-2001.2011.01206.x

Hauerwas, S., & Pinches, C. (1997). *Christians among the virtues: Theological conversations with ancient and modern ethics.* University of Notre Dame Press.

Herdt, J. (2015). Varieties of contemporary Christian virtue ethics. In L. Besser-Jones & M. Slote (Eds.), *The Routledge companion to virtue ethics* (pp. 223–236).

Jackson, T. (2003). *The priority of love: Christian love and social justice.* Princeton Univesrity Press.

Jacobs, N. L., & Richardson, R. (2022). *At the gates: Disability, justice, and the churches.* Darton, Longman & Todd Ltd.

Komeda, H., Kosaka, H., Saito, D., Mano, Y., Jung, M., Fujii, T., Yanaka, H., Munesue, T., Ishitobi, M., Sato, M., & Okazawa, H. (2015). Autistic empathy toward autistic others. *Social Cognitive and Affective Neuroscience*, 10(2), 145–152. https://doi.org/10.1093/scan/nsu126

Kristjansson, K. (2020). Aristotelian character friendship as a 'method' of moral education. *Studies in Philosophy and Education*, 39(4), 349–364. https://doi.org/10.1007/s11217-020-09717-w

Livingston, L., Colvert, E., Bolton, P., & Happe, F. (2019). Good social skills despite poor theory of mind: Exploring compensation in autism spectrum disorder. *Journal of Child Psychology and Psychiatry, and Allied Disciplines*, 60(1), 102–110. https://doi.org/10.1111/jcpp.12886

Markram, H., Rinaldi, T., & Markram, K. (2007). The intense world syndrome – An alternative hypothesis for autism. *Frontiers in Neuroscience*, 1(1), 77–96. https://doi.org/10.3389/neuro.01.1.1.006.2007

Markram, K., & Markram, H. (2010). The Intense world theory – A unifying theory of the neurobiology of autism. *Frontiers in Human Neuroscience, 4*(224), 224. https://doi.org/10.3389/fnhum.2010.00224

McLaren, K. (2013). *The art of empathy: A complete guide to life's most essential skill.* Sounds True.

Milton, D. E. (2012). On the ontological status of autism: The 'double empathy' problem. *Disability & Society, 27*(6), 883–887. https://doi.org/10.1080/09687599.2012.710008

MacIntyre, A. (2016). *Ethics in the conflicts of modernity: An essay on desire, practical reasoning, and narrative.* Cambridge University Press.

Myers, N. A. L. (2016). Recovery stories: An anthropological exploration of moral agency in stories of mental health recovery. *Transcultural Psychiatry, 53*(4), 427–444. https://doi.org/10.1177/1363461516663124

Nothwehr, D. M. (2016). Bonaventure of Bagnoregio's Imatatio Christi as an agapistic virtue ethics. In D. V. Meconi (Ed.), *On earth as it is in heaven: Cultivating a contemporary theology of creation* (pp. 123–145). Catholic University of America Press.

Premack, D., & Woodruff, G. (1978). Does the chimpanzee have a theory of mind? *Behavioral and Brain Sciences, 1*(4), 515–526. https://doi.org/10.1017/S0140525X00076512

Pripas-Kapit, S. (2020). Historicizing Jim Sinclair's 'don't mourn for us': A cultural and intellectual history of neurodiversity's first manifesto. In S.K. Kapp (Ed.), *Autistic community and the neurodiversity movement* (pp. 23–38). Palgrave Macmillan. https://doi.org/10.1007/978-981-13-8437-0_2

Reinders, H. S. (2008). *Receiving the gift of friendship: Profound disability, theological anthropology, and ethics.* William B Eerdmans Press.

Rosello, B., Berenguer, C., Baixauli, I., Garcia, R., & Miranda, A. (2020). Theory of mind profiles in children with autism spectrum disorder: Adaptive/social skills and pragmatic competence. *Frontiers in Psychology, 11,* 567401. https://doi.org/10.3389/fpsyg.2020.567401

Sinclair, J. (2012). "Don't Mourn for Us." *Autonomy, the Critical Journal of Interdisciplinary Autism Studies.* Original work published in Our Voice 1.3 (1993), the Autism Network International newsletter. https://philosophy.ucsc.edu/SinclairDontMournForUs.pdf, accessed May 15, 2023.

Snow, N. E. (2010). *Virtue as social intelligence: An empirically grounded theory.* Routledge Books.

Sheppard, E., Pillai, D., Tze-Lynn Wong, G., Ropar, D., & Mitchell, P. (2016). How easy is it to read the minds of people with autism spectrum disorder? *Journal of Autism and Developmental Disorders, 46*(4), 1247–1254. https://doi.org/10.1007/s10803-015-2662-8

Shoemaker, D. (2015). *Responsibility from the margins.* Oxford University Press.

Sterponi, L. (2004). Construction of rules, accountability and moral identity by high-functioning children with autism. *Discourse Studies, 6*(2), 207–228. https://doi.org/10.1177/1461445604041768

Swinton, J. (2012). Reflections on autistic love: What does love look like? *Practical Theology, 5*(3), 259–278. https://doi.org/10.1558/prth.v5i3.259

Williams, B. A. O., Nagel, T. (1976). *Proceedings of the Aristotelian Society 50: 115-135 and 137-151.* https://doi.org/10.1093/aristoteliansupp/50.1.115

Zagzebski, L. (2017). *Exemplarist moral theory.* Oxford University Press.

Zimmerman, M. J. (2015). Moral luck reexamined. In David Shoemaker (Ed.), *Oxford studies in agency and responsibility* (Vol. 3, pp. 136–159). Oxford University Press.

Dismantling the Supercrip Prof: Theological Education and Faculty Accessibility

Natalie Wigg-Stevenson

ABSTRACT

Most research around neurodiversity in higher education focuses on students, with little attention paid to faculty. This essay deploys autoethnographic narratives to (a) ground anti-ableist pedagogy in decolonizing pedagogy; (b) argue that cognitive- and neuro-diversity among faculty should be valued similarly to—and in intersection with—other forms of diversity, (c) explore barriers to disclosure among disabled, chronically ill and neurodivergent faculty, and (d) call for a structural approach to anti-ableism in theological education that not only accommodates disabled, chronically ill and neurodivergent faculty needs, but also scales up those accommodations to create a workplace environment in which all faculty can flourish.

Even though, my "Context, Power and Coloniality" course only has eight students registered, I still request our largest lecture hall for its meetings. Not because I lecture—but, rather, because we move around a lot. So, we need a lot of space.

"Could we meet less often, but for longer chunks of time, please?" I ask our registrar, requesting an irregular schedule of four six-hour long meetings rather than the standard twelve two-hour long ones. "Ok," she says, "but you'll have to meet on Fridays when no one else is around." *Totally worth it*, I think. What's the point of having extra space to move if you don't also have extra time to move slowly?

Each class opens with five minutes of silence, as we circle around a table with candles, a singing bowl, and snacks. We return to this circle throughout the day, whenever we need to feel grounded again. I also place printed lists of the day's learning outcomes on a table near the room's exit so students can leave notes about what they are and aren't understanding as they come and go. I use these notes to adjust the day's lesson plans accordingly.

Across the semester, we'll read the minimal amount required to support our learning. I'm not at all bothered about covering a canon, even a re-imagined one. This approach lets students maintain their own pace and/or go down rabbit holes of their own interest. We spend the entire last day working together to equip students to use their final paper to integrate their course learning with their own social location and vocational context. And we'll use an adaptive mix of individual and group work as well as one-on-one coaching to keep everyone working at their own growing edges. We also leave the semester's final three weeks completely empty of assigned readings, writing or meeting. That way, every student can work on their final project at their own pace. And finally, for students who have a hard time finding that pace, we also have optional check-in and benchmark feedback moments in their paper writing process to support them staying on track.

We also do different activities in this class that involve arranging, organizing and labeling the room and its furniture to create spatial representations of the concepts with which we're working. It sounds weird, but it works. This past term, one activity required that I draw a conceptual map on the floor out of painter's tape—which I immediately drew upside down. Or maybe inside-out. The fact is that, despite wanting to use the space to teach concepts in embodied ways, I'm actually terrible at spatial reasoning. So, I asked the students who are skilled at such things to fix it while the rest of us milled about. Then I jumped back in to tell the story of the concept the map represented—because while I'm not good at spatial reasoning, I am good at storytelling.

"You can walk the map," I told the students, "to gain a bodily understanding of how you relate to this concept." Most then walked the map slowly, labyrinth style. But one man dashed quickly back and forth across it with his hands clasped tightly behind his back. He was the last to find his landing spot. We all waited. We're comfortable being out of step with each other. Then we all sat on the floor, or pulled up chairs, or shuffled back and forth in place wherever we had landed to share with each other how our bodies knew where to stop moving and what we learned about ourselves once we got there.

Universal design for whom?

What follows is heavily autoethnographic.[1] It arises from my social location as, among other things, a scholar seeking to integrate diagnoses of bi-polar disorder, generalized anxiety disorder, and ADHD into her professional and personal sense of self and who is, at this time of writing, in recovery from a traumatic brain injury. Like my students, I need five minutes of silence to calm my overactive nervous system when I arrive to class. Even with that meditation moment, though, I'll still get overexcited and talk too quickly as class moves along. And that will cause an anxious rumination spiral over whether what I've said has made sense. Giving the students a chance to offer me ongoing feedback about their learning helps stop that spiral. Fidgeting also helps me to focus, because a lot of excess energy builds up in my body while I teach. So, being able to walk around a map on the floor or among different conversation stations keeps me in my teaching/learning zone. But it took me a while to realize how—or, even, why—all this was working so well for me too.

My initial pedagogical design for "Context, Power and Coloniality" grew out of a desire to contribute to practices of decolonizing theological education. To dismantle (or, perhaps, at best chip away at) the colonizing structures and practices of academic knowledge requires more than just decentering a Western European canon of texts in any given discipline. The problem isn't just the dominance of Western *knowledge*; the problem is how dominant Western *ways of knowing* "render alternative [global] knowledge traditions irrelevant and invisible" (O'Donovan, 2010, 171). Colonizing ways of knowing divide and conquer: mind from and over body, the knower from and over the person, the expert from and over the novice, the individual from and over the collective. Decolonizing pedagogical practice has to start, therefore, by seeking to center and normalize ways of knowing that resist and heal these rifts.

As the learning design of the "Context" course attempted this resistance and healing—i.e., through practices that seek to reintegrate mind/body and knower/person, value the wisdom spoken at each stage of a learning journey and attend to how the learning experiences of individuals and the experience of the collective interact—I noticed my neurodivergent students start to open up more. By shifting the colonial structures that limit cultural epistemological diversity, we'd somehow shifted the ableist structures that limit cognitive epistemological diversity as well. And the more I slowed things down in our class, the more I saw how Riyad A. Shahjahan's call to practice "being lazy" in ways that disrupt obsessively-measured dynamics of colonial time and Alison Kafer's articulation of "crip time" as a way to "challenge normative and normalizing expectations of pace and scheduling," are both fighting different heads of the same expansive hydra (Kafer, 2013; Shahjahan, 2015).

As neurodivergent students' sense of belonging increased, so too did their desire to contribute to shaping not just our classroom conversations, but also our classroom culture. Where their contributions cohered with *my* decolonizing goals and practices, I was ready to collaborate. Not ever having any learning accommodations myself, however, or knowing much at all about accessible pedagogy, I failed to even perceive any contributions they made that didn't directly cohere with what I was already doing. Rightly frustrated, their contributions turned to critique. As an anonymous student comment on one of my course evaluations read, "She needs incorporate UDL[2] into her pedagogy."[3] As another one put it, "For someone who purports to care about justice, she sure is ableist!"

I was meeting the students' accommodations, but I hadn't recognized that they needed these accommodations because my overall learning design was only inadvertently (rather than intentionally) more accessible. It's also the case that not all accommodations manage to address the barriers precisely as students experience them.[4] Accessibility services are necessary because inaccessible design is simply presumed in higher education. Just as professors aren't required to decolonize our classroom practices, we're also not required to use UDL. Those of us who do these things *above and beyond* what's *required* do so because we're ethically committed to them. This means that oftentimes the cost of student wellness gets withdrawn from the already depleted faculty wellness bank. Moreover, those of us committed to making learning accessible are often committed to it because we're disabled, chronically ill, or neurodivergent ourselves—which makes the wellness withdrawal all the more significant.[5]

The same colonial and ableist systems that create barriers to learners learning also create barriers to educators educating. Our students know that accommodations are stopgap measures on the road to creating more accessible design. But, as I'll outline below, most faculty who need workplace accommodations don't even pursue—or even think about pursuing—them. So we definitely don't pursue advocating for overall accessibility in our institutional design. We just keep pretending things will be better next semester when x, y or z isn't on our plate anymore. In this article, then, I argue that theological educators who have taken our students' accessibility needs seriously also need to start taking seriously our own…perhaps even need to *first* take seriously our own.

I'm struck at how selfish I feel writing that…which is exactly why it needs to be written. Overwhelmed by my student's request for UDL, I simply ignored it for a while. I couldn't even entertain it before I'd figured out the plane was going down and I needed to get my oxygen mask on first. And at that point, I could finally begin to see that the solution is not to step back from universal design, but rather to expand it—not just as a set of teaching strategies but, rather, as tool to reimagine—perhaps even to crip—the whole theological institution in ways that make flourishing possible for all its students, staff, faculty and administrators alike.

Please (don't really) ask me for anything!

Before I got the care I needed, though—that is, before I could start taking neurodiversity seriously at the structural level of my pedagogical approach—I tried some ad hoc measures, particularly in how I did the accessibility portion of the first day of class, syllabus read-through.

"We're committed to supporting everyone's learning here," I said the first time I tried this. Pause: make sure they'd absorbed the institutional commitment. "...but I'm also personally committed." I'm not gonna screw you guys over. In fact, I want to go above and beyond for you..., "so, please, please let me know if you need anything. My door is always open."

The vagueness of offering "anything" came back to bite me one summer, though, as the previous academic year's admin overload overflow began competing with the next academic year's admin overload trying to get a head start. I'd already been working throughout the vacation time I was supposed to take (because, no one actually takes it, and I didn't want to be the only jerk who did—no matter how much my kids begged to me to put down my laptop and play with them).[6] "I can't do it anymore," I sobbed to my therapist, sometime toward the end of July, "I'm just too tired."

You're not tired, Natalie," she said. "You're burned out. And if you...

There's nothing to do!" I wailed, cutting her off. "You don't understand my job! I'm the slacker on the team!!

I don't know what everyone else at your workplace does, Natalie. I just know what you need to do.

So, I did something I'd never done before: I planned a solo overnight retreat during the last few days before school was going to get going again. My therapist had recommended four to seven days: *but she doesn't know me*, I told myself, *I don't need four days, I can do it in two* ...knowing full well I'd cut it back to a day—at most, a day and a half—when all was said and done.

Then, a couple of days before I was set to leave, a student emailed me to say that their life had fallen apart—and, due to the particular courses they still needed to graduate, I was the only person on faculty who could help them out.

Surely not, I thought.

But after assessing their situation, I realized they were right. And there wasn't enough time left in the summer for me to help them *and* go off the grid for a day and a half (maybe a day...or just an afternoon).

I remember you telling us we could ask you for *anything* when we found ourselves in trouble," the student said, "and I'm in trouble.

I cancelled the retreat.

As the fall term got going, both this student's mental health and mine declined sharply. Desperate, the student rallied their fellow students to send a formal letter to the faculty letting us know we weren't supporting them as they felt we should. "This is *theological* education!" they said. "The faculty should *care* more," we were told. "You guys are just beholden to the neo-liberal capitalist bottom line."

It broke me.

Don't care?! I fumed. *Do you guys have any idea what I've sacrificed for you??*

But, of course, they didn't—because they would have assumed that the professor teaching them about professional boundaries would be better at setting her own.

***

I had offered my students "anything" because I'd seen their accommodations fail them. Piling ad hoc solutions on top of their stop gap measures let me act out some Dead Poets' fantastical self-image twist: I got to be the "cool prof" who broke the rules so that genuine learning could happen—without ever acknowledging my institutional privilege that those rules were there to protect me. I could retreat behind them whenever I wanted—at least, in theory.

Indeed, that was the problem: the rules were there to protect me from students' needs, not to support me in meeting those needs. I could either hide behind them or over-extend myself breaking them. But to create the space to be able to meet students' needs *and* survive—dare I say, flourish—would require more mutual teacher-student vulnerability than academic institutions typically encourage, or even permit.

Once I realized this, I spent a few terms' first-day syllabus read-throughs highlighting our accessibility policy and then ad-libbing something like: "Everyone is legally entitled to the accommodations they secure through accessibility services. But, for those who want to explore more tailored access to their learning, I'm happy to meet and strategize with you about that. I live with mental illness...and that's why this is important to me!"

This approach brought more students out of the woodwork for support. It also gave me some cover to set my own boundaries as I extended myself beyond the legal accessibility requirements. But by disclosing some vague version of my own health conditions, I was now performing both prof-in-solidarity *and* inspiring super-crip-scholar.[7] "Look at me, guys! I've made it...and with my help, so too can you!"

By this point, I was dealing with some new diagnoses and their concurrent new treatment and pharmacological regimes. Things had gotten dire enough that I finally had no other choice than to request workplace accommodations for myself—which I once again tried to do in an ad hoc way: *maybe*, I thought, *if I just told my department head what was going on, they could quietly take a few things of my plate. No one has to know.* My internalized stigma led me to hedge around my needs, which made my request so unclear and, frankly, awkward that I'm deeply grateful to this day my department head just sent me to Human Resources to work the whole thing out over there instead.

Of course, at the time, I griped to my friends and family: "This is theological education. My supervisor should care more. But I guess admin is just too beholden to the neo-liberal capitalist bottom line." Sound familiar?

***

Research out of the UK shows that while 16% of working-age adults and nearly 13% of undergraduates report having a disability, only 3.9% of university academics report the same (Brown & Leigh, 2018). In the US, a survey of faculty who self-identified as having "mental disabilities, mental illness or mental-health histories" found that nearly 70% knew little to nothing about their accommodation options within their university, and only 13% had ever requested accommodations (Price et al., 2017).

Further research also shows that even when disabled, chronically ill and neurodivergent faculty do pursue accommodations and, even, experience some supportive moments during our disclosure process, we still experience overwhelming forms of stigma and discrimination that make the overall experience much more difficult than it need be. Those negative moments stay with us, producing an ongoing sense of fear and stress alongside—perhaps, as an undertow to—how accessible our accommodations can actually make our work become (Mellifont, 2023). If we're not up for the long haul of self-advocacy, it really feels like it's best not to try at all.[8]

The data parallels my own experience, which, while perfectly average, still took a significant toll. I had to do more advocacy for myself for adequate Human Resources support than standard—let alone, best—practices recommend. And it took months for my requests to be heard, let alone accommodated. Various meetings to implement my accommodations with management entailed a (certainly unintentional, but nevertheless real) process by which my experience was minimized, stigmatized and shamed. I also had to and will continue to have to go through this stressful experience again each time management changes.

Perhaps the most stressful part of requiring a workplace accommodation for me, though, is that within our egalitarian academic context—where faculty workload is more self- than other-governed—I am the one who is responsible for ensuring that any accommodations I negotiate with management are adhered to when faculty decide who will be taking on which tasks among us.[9] But, if I'm working forty hours a week and everyone else is working sixty plus, how can I possibly do my "fair share" of what we've together deemed needs doing?[10]

When I say "no," my overburdened colleagues get more overburdened. And I'm left looking at their attempt to hide their frustration while I quickly discern among: (1) my privacy protections = don't give a reason = look like a terrible team player; (2) offer a vague self-disclosure that I have an "accommodation" = raise suspicions that I might be crazy; or (3) do a full self-disclosure = confirm suspicions that I'm crazy.[11] It takes a toll.

Given how desperate I had to get to pursue accommodations, I do wonder how many faculty spend their careers just slightly on the other side of desperation's fine line. It should go without saying (but frankly, I don't think it does): something slightly better than desperation just isn't good enough. So, while this essay's main goal is to convince theological education administrators to implement more universally designed approaches to faculty workload and wellness, I suspect that won't happen until more faculty who are entitled to workplace accommodations get them, and then use them strategically to disrupt the overall system. This essay's secondary goal, therefore, is to convince more faculty who could get workplace accommodations to do so—even if that means simply having their regional labor laws put into writing on their behalf.

From performative solidarity to genuine need

This brings me to my most recent iteration of first-day syllabus read-through accessibility policy unpacking. For the "Context, Power and Coloniality" course I describe above, I maintained the standard legal template that we're all required to include:

> *Accessibility. Students with a disability or health consideration, whether temporary or permanent, are entitled to accommodation. Students in conjoint degree programs must register at the University of Toronto's Accessibility Services offices; information is available at http://www.studentlife.utoronto.ca/as The sooner a student seeks accommodation, the quicker we can assist. Students who have supplied accessibility documentation may request pre-approval at the start of term to submit all journal entries on alternative specific dates during the term.*

But then, I added the paragraph:

> *The course instructor also has accessibility requirements. Students supplying accessibility documentation do not need to consider the instructor's needs when making requests covered by their approved accommodations. Students who wish to strategize how to manage their needs in relation to their learning in a more holistic way are welcome to discuss further adjustments to course requirements with the instructor. In such cases, we will find a mutually agreed upon approach that takes into account both of our health needs.*

If I hadn't called attention to that second paragraph, I doubt students would have even noticed it. But putting into writing what I had recently only been ad-libbing felt like a hugely vulnerable step to me.

This written change shifted the line for engagement, reconstituting what I ad-libbed as a more specific disclosure. "I live with a bi-polar diagnosis," I said, "that I'm still trying to integrate into my sense of self. And I have to structure my work life (as well as my daily life) very carefully to ensure my wellbeing as I do that integration."[12] I then explained that I had designed the course outcomes, assessments, expectations, and activities using UDL principles—meaning that fewer "accommodations" should (at least, in principle) be necessary, but that all legal accommodations would certainly be met. "But I also have my own workplace accommodations," I added, "... my workload is reduced to 40 h per week and I get time for lunch and pee breaks" (I paused to let that sink in for those with aspirations to academia).

By shifting from performative solidarity to expressing a genuine state of need, I wanted them to know I'm committed to going "above and beyond" with care for those who need it, but that going "above and beyond" for everyone is something of which I'm not capable. In other words: *we've got a tricky situation here, and I'm not the only one responsible for resolving it.*

> "We're going to be talking a lot about power and privilege in this class," I said, "and my hope is that we can create a community of care that lets us all learn these things in a real way. So, from the outset, I'm asking students who don't require accommodations to structure your term carefully so that you don't need to ask for extensions based on your poor time management." They bristled a bit at that. I didn't back down. "But really, plot your semester and work in advance. If you've got three papers due at the same time *and* you have neurotypical executive functioning, set dates on your calendar to start working on those papers earlier." They laughed. "Rather than just *checking* your neurotypical privilege," I suggested, "I invite you to consider using it to benefit those of us who are neurodivergent."

I'm not a supercrip prof. I want to be able to go above and beyond (whatever that means) for the students who—due to how who they are intersects with the unjust ways our institutions operate—require more support. And I want to provide enough support that these students not only survive or even thrive, but can actually help co-create more just ways for our programs to work. But I don't have that much support to give. I need others to do it with me.

By and large, this approach worked—at least so far.[13] Students set their own goals to stretch their capacities without overextending themselves. And I felt mostly able to keep up with whatever got thrown my way. And, here's the kicker: the students wrote the best papers I've ever seen in any iteration of this course across twelve years of teaching it. The quantity of work we did was much less than usual. The quality of learning we experienced was much higher—because the practice/theory, action/reflection aspects of the course were continually running side by side. Students were learning theory that they were being asked to live, and they were practicing participating in a community justly with theoretical resources to help them unpack their intuitions for doing so as they were doing it. By the time it came to write their papers, they'd already done so much integrative learning, they were starting past the finish line of where the race is usually run.

So, if this approach has the potential to work so well for both students and faculty, then why did it take me so long to figure it out, and what are the barriers to other faculty trying it too? The only reason I could take this particular step to foster a classroom culture of mutual responsibility and care was because my own accommodations were already on-record through my Human Resources department—a move we've already seen most faculty feel they can't make. I certainly wouldn't have felt safe doing so before I got tenure.[14] But, we shouldn't have to be burned out beyond capacity before we can ask for help. We shouldn't have to be burned out beyond capacity at all.

Hands Up if You're Flourishing!

At a recent faculty meeting, we were trying to figure out how to tackle a specific delimited curricular problem. We then deliberated over each potential solution's implications for our students. Each implication then proliferated further problems for an already overwhelmed faculty's to-do list…thus proliferating further solutions and implications and so on. Until eventually, what started as a single problem had rapidly become an interlocking system of equally urgent needs.

Instead of pulling that system apart to assign different priorities to different tasks, however, someone at the table simply said, "so who is able to take this on right now?"

I wondered aloud if we should consider the workload impact that attempting to do everything on the list would have on our faculty community. "Perhaps we should prioritize some items, while—even though we know it's not perfect—letting others go," I tried.

A colleague responded, "yes, we should consider our own potential for human flourishing here, right? Isn't 'flourishing' a thing that theologians care about?"

I didn't have time to ask if this colleague was intending to make a joke, because everyone else was already laughing. Then someone else then quipped, "hands up if you're flourishing!"

My hand was already halfway lifted as the laughter grew louder still, and I felt a visceral sensation of shame emerge from my gut, flood through my shoulder, past my wrist and into my half-raised hand—paralyzing any further movement. I use this potentially ableist term on purpose: my colleagues' laughter *disabled* me.[15] So, I couldn't say the very thing that I wanted to say—*I'm flourishing. I mean, at least today, I'm feeling like I might be flourishing. Besides, I deserve to flourish. And you do too!*—because saying so would have exposed me.

If I'm flourishing or, even, nearly flourishing, then it must be at someone else's expense. At least, that's the lie the system tells us. It's also a lie I refuse to keep telling, and I want others to stop telling it too.

***

As higher education increasingly strives to re-imagine its practices with regards to equity, diversity and inclusion, the focus has thus far been on cultivating diversity along lines of gender, sexuality, race and ethnicity—and rightly so. Still, given the intersectional nature of how diverse epistemologies operate, an academic context that strives for a truly inclusive practice needs to create the conditions for cognitive and neurodiversity as well—not only among its students, but among its faculty and administrators too.

Unfortunately, the Euro-Western structures that undergird academic knowledge production generate norms and values that perceive neurodivergence as a problem to be fixed or accommodated rather than a possibility to be celebrated and mobilized. Just as some scholars' neurotypicality causes them to struggle in some areas and offer contributions in others, though, so too does other scholars' neurodivergence. We don't want everyone in academia to think *the same things*. So, why do we expect us all to think *in the same way*?

As we already know, if we want to diversify a faculty, we must hire people from diverse constituencies *and* create the structural conditions for their flourishing. So, while I would love to see theological schools begin intentionally recruiting neurodivergent faculty members, we must also start creating the conditions for such faculty's flourishing within our daily practices now. Besides, we already have disabled, chronically ill, and neurodivergent people serving on our faculties.[16] If we think we don't, we need to ask ourselves what we're doing to make it unsafe for our colleagues to self-disclose. So, if leaders in theological education developed policies and practices that made accommodations possible without requiring disclosure, as Margaret Price and their colleagues argue we should do, then we could begin creating a culture in which current neurodivergent faculty were supported *and* new neurodivergent faculty could be recruited (Price et al., 2017). This would go a long way toward dismantling ableism in theological education.

But theologians care about so much more than dismantling evils. We also purport to promote flourishing—the thing my faculty says we want for others but finds hilarious for ourselves. As higher education specialists Brown, Thompson and Leigh argue, the kinds of accommodations that benefit disabled, chronically ill and neurodivergent scholars could benefit all and should, therefore, be made available to all (Brown et al., 2018). To dismantle ableism *and* promote flourishing in theological education at all levels, administrators need to develop a "culture of access" that "emphasiz[es and fosters] collective accountability" (Price et al., 2017). For example, I shouldn't have been the only one in my faculty meeting to suggest that we prioritize some tasks over others to ensure our shared wellness. That should be a question we all ask each other—and, if we don't, our leadership should remind us—every time we're deciding whether or not to take on something new.[17]

Just as we've learned that when we challenge the sexism, misogyny, colonialism, racism and heteronormativity that pervades academia we produce a better workplace culture for all, so too we need to realize that challenging ableism in higher education can disrupt the cycle of overwork's normalization that impedes all of our flourishing. Moreover, because we now know that those most marginalized can't dismantle the structures that marginalize them alone, we need enabled/temporarily abled and disabled, neurotypical and neurodivergent, chronically and only sometimes ill faculty to work together to create the kinds of inclusive practice we all purport to want.

If isolation is a key contributor to why faculty don't disclose their conditions and related needs regarding accessibility, then relationships are what's key to creating the structural change required for everyone's mutual flourishing. "Meaningful access," Aimi Hamraie argues, is a form of "relational accountability" that is "learned through interaction and materialized through reciprocal encounters" (Hamraie, 2016, 265–266). Meaningful access isn't something you *think*; it's something you *feel*—which is probably why it's so difficult for academics to create, shaped as we are by colonizing and neuronormalizing ways of knowing that prioritize thinking over feeling (Price et al., 2017). But developing an imagination for future hope is what theologians are all about! Moreover, theologians tend to believe that the not yet of a future hope is somehow also already here—if not as something we can understand, then as something we can experience. So, who better than us to feel our way into a new imagination for dismantling ableism in theological education? Who better than us to create a new beloved community in which we can generate our mutual flourishing together?[18]

Notes

1. Autoethnographers use their personal experiences to bring wider cultural practices into view in ways that critique those practices *and* seek to transform them. While often dismissed as solipsistic, autoethnography has the potential to illuminate the affective, experiential dynamics of cultural practices. Its goal is less to convince the reader to think differently using an argument, and more to compel the reader to act differently using a story. Autoethnography therefore disrupts and re-configures dominant academic epistemologies; hence its inclusion in my scholarly toolkit. For more on autoethnography see: Adams et al., 2022; Ellis & Bochner, 2006; Holman Jones et al., 2013; Walford, 2021; Wigg-Stevenson, 2017).

2. UDL stands for "Universal Design for Learning," an approach that provides learners with multiple means of *engagement*, *representation*, *action* and *expression* in the learning process so that they *access*, *build*, and *internalize* their learning in ways that activate their *affective*, *recognition* and *strategic* networks. Its goal is to make learning accessible for *all learners*. Where learning is not accessible, learners require learning *accommodations* to have equitable *access* to their learning.

3. I should admit that I didn't know what UDL was when I received these comments. As I scoured articles about these techniques on the internet, I came across multiple graphics that summarize UDL's core principles. These graphics made me physically nauseous because the amount of information they conveyed overwhelmed me. Put differently, my students' frustrations didn't just start my journey to learn about neurodiversity: their frustrations began my journey to learning I was neurodivergent!

4. The most common version of this that I have experienced is when a student who has ADHD is given an extra week to *finish* their assignment. But when that student's particular executive function struggle is around *starting* their assignment, the extra week actually makes things worse for them. For me to be able to support them in ways that actually improves their learning access and, even, potentially equips them with the skills required to manage their own learning processes better, would require they disclose their condition to me—which is precisely what Accessibility Services protects them from having to do. This isn't Accessibility Services' fault. They are also overworked, understaffed, underfunded and often doing the best they can in a wider university context that is oriented more towards legal compliance when it comes to disability than actual student care.

5. Throughout this essay, I use a blend of person-first language, identity-first language, language related to the medical model for disability and even the pathologizing paradigm, as well as language related to the social disability model to refer to myself. I have made each choice in context to convey something particular about my experience. When speaking in general, though, and despite the more common use of person-first language in disability theology, I will use identity-first language like enabled and disabled, neurotypical and neurodivergent people, following Nick Walker's critique (see https://neuroqueer.com/person-first-language-is-the-language-of-autistiphobic-bigots/).

6. Brown and Leigh link academics' tendency to minimize/avoid using their vacation time and/or sick leave with how values of research, teaching and good institutional citizenship get deployed to normalize overwork. Research shows that while "academics with disabilities or illnesses work hard to hold onto their academic work and identity whilst compromising other aspects of their life...non-academic individuals with similar health challenges reported that work was the first thing they dropped to maintain their personal lives and relationships." (Brown & Leigh, 2018: 986–987).

Further, while we don't yet have hard data on academic versus non-academic rates of divorce, the significant anecdotal evidence has led to more people calling for research into the relationship between academic workloads, gender and marital dissolution (Boufis, 1999).

7. The term, 'supercrip' was coined by disability advocate and writer, Eli Clare, to demonstrate two forms of ableism: one everyday and one exceptional. For the everyday version, wider society interprets disability as a challenge to overcome, and thus interprets people with disabilities as superheroes—simply for living their lives. At the same time, wider society might only value people with disabilities when they're able to demonstrate the exceptional as a source of inspiration for nondisabled people (e.g., climbing Everest, world leader in theoretical physics, running across Canada with one leg while dying of cancer). See Eli Clare, "The Mountain," in (Clare, 2015).

8. As my psychiatrist was writing my accessibility support letter, she had me practice the phrases: "I want to succeed at/be excellent at my job," and "My psychiatrist says these are the accommodations I need to meet all the expectations of and/or excel in the workplace." She warned me not [to] link the accommodations in any way to my own survival or wellness. "And definitely don't mention your kids," she added. I use these phrases in every accommodations-related meeting I have. They are the best advice I have to offer to other scholars seeking to secure their own accommodations. Frame every request with the way it helps you serve the institution. And practice your framing before any meeting. Because it's going to feel awful to prioritize the institution over your own wellness as you try to secure your own survival. My other advice is not to underplay your needs—which my psychiatrist noted I was doing. I insisted that I wasn't, but realize now that I was lying to her and to myself. I was afraid to ask for "too much." Disabled, neurodivergent, and chronically ill people are always afraid of asking for or being "too much." We have to stop that.

9. It's worth noting here, that my personal 'accommodations' are actually just a formal re-statement of the provincial labor laws where I live. Indeed, it was difficult to explain to my psychiatrist and human resources representative why my only chance of having a forty hour work week, daily thirty minute lunch breaks plus two other fifteen-minute breaks, and personal time to attend medical appointments (I didn't even bother trying to ask for formal sick days) would be to request it via the Accessible Canada Act (ACA, Canada's equivalent to the ADA), rather than via the provincial labour laws that already guaranteed it.

10. A pre-pandemic, non-scientific study of Canadian professors found that we work an average of 48 hours per week (Brownell, 2018), a number that increased by at least 10 hours per week during the pandemic (Austin-Smith, 2020). Attending to the US (where the faculty workload situation is more bleak than in already-bleak Canada), a survey conducted by MIT in 2001 compared university faculty and CEOs regarding workload questions. 78% of faculty reported that "no matter how hard they work, they can't get everything done" whereas on 48% of CEOs said the same. Furthermore, 62% of faculty reported "feeling physically or emotionally drained at the end of the day" compared to 55% of CEOs ((Berg & Seeber, 2016: pg. 16).

11. I recognize that the terminology "crazy" can be ableist. It can also be reclaimed as empowering, which some of us in the "mad" community are doing. I use it here to self-describe because it's one of the ways I identify. I would not, however, use it to describe anyone who hasn't intentionally claimed it for themselves.

12. I wasn't diagnosed with ADHD until halfway through the term when I taught this course, at which point I shared about that in ad hoc ways as well whenever it felt

relevant to our shared teaching and learning.

13. The process of writing this article helped me figure out how to articulate and transfer these decolonizing, crip approaches into my redesign of the MDiv Integrative Seminar I am teaching this semester. They are even more interwoven into the structural pedagogical design of the course now, which has led me to move them from the syllabus' 'accessibility' portion into the course and assignment descriptions—syllabus sections that the students and I have begun to refer to as "Natalie's pedagogical manifesto" for shorthand.

14. I wish I had good news or even just advice for specifically junior scholars here trying to navigate these same systems. I've only been tenured for about five years, but the precarity my generation faced seems like the golden years now compared to what post-pandemic junior scholars in theological education are dealing with. Particularly concerning is that by the point of tenure in an academic career, we've so internalized the propensity to overwork that it's difficult to recognize our role in reproducing overwork's normalization for each other and for the next generation. This is why it's so important for those of us who do have institutional security not only to try to change these oppressive systems, but also to find ways to provide safe cover for junior colleagues navigating them as they're currently rigged.

15. Whereas a medical model for understanding disability sees a bodily impairment as a problem to be solved, a social model for understanding disability interprets the social conditions that make it impossible for people with impairments to flourish as the problem. So, whatever made my colleagues laugh are the same social conditions that make our shared flourishing impossible. And it's those social conditions that need to change.

16. A number that will surely increase thanks to the growing phenomena of Long-COVID and Post-Covid conditions.

17. I should note that after sharing the draft of this article with our leadership, conversations in my context seem to be opening up. I'm hopeful!

18. One of the peer reviewers for this article rightly pointed out that it ends on the desire for flourishing without theologizing what flourishing is. I agree with the reviewer that the article would be strengthened if I did that theological work. Instead of strengthening the article, though, I'm going to leave it just a little bit weak: not out of performative solidarity, but out of genuine need.

    I could just ignore the reviewer's excellent suggestion. No one would have known. But I do have just enough energy to write this footnote.

    Yesterday I discerned that some institutionally marginalized students required 'above and beyond' care. Offering that care took an emotional and physical toll on me that I'm paying for today—the day I set aside to deal with the 'flourishing edits'. I'm also close to my accommodated 40 hours for this week, this article is due, and I don't want to make more work for this journal issue's editors by missing the deadline.

    Knowing about my brain injury (which makes dealing with words difficult), Erin Rafferty, one of those editors, extended the generous offer to help me get it across the finish line. She has a lot on her plate too, though, so I wanted to find a way *not* to take her up on it. So, here I must extend gratitude to my writing group (Colleen Shantz, Michael O'Conner and Reid Locklin, especially Reid) who gave me emotional and intellectual support, as well as specific line edit feedback on this article's penultimate draft, and to my research assistant Mike MacKenzie who proofread it for me. Their support let me finish up without Erin's help. It takes a (neurodiverse) village!

I don't intend this footnote to set a precedent for authors just to articulate why they didn't get everything done *or* just to shove what they didn't get to into a note at the end of an article. But, I would direct the reader to the Canadian Journal of Theology, Mental Health, and Disability, where their experimentation with neuro-affirming forms of academic publishing has led them to include questions for readers to ponder at the end of their articles.

And then, I would remind the reader that this paper already contains multiple stories that illustrate the "relational accountability" required for "meaningful access" playing about across the power differentials of a teacher and students who got to feel that not yet future hope before we thought it. It would also explain that the purpose of autoethnography isn't to construct an argument that convinces the reader of a new idea but, rather, its purpose is to tell stories that compel the reader towards a new action. And I would ask you: what might the already not yet version of flourishing look like for you?

Disclosure statement

No potential conflict of interest was reported by the author(s).

References

Adams, T. E., Holman Jones, S. L., & Ellis, C. (2022). *Handbook of autoethnography* (Second edition.). Routledge.

Austin-Smith, B. (2020, December 18). The impact of the pandemic on academic workers and work. *The Canadian Experience.*

Berg, M., & Seeber, B. K. (2016). *The slow professor: Challenging the culture of speed in the academy.* University of Toronto Press.

Boufis, C. (1999, March 25). Strange bedfellows: Does academic life lead to divorce? *Salon.* https://www.salon.com/1999/03/25/24feature_5/.

Brown, N., & Leigh, J. (2018). Ableism in academia: Where are the disabled and ill academics? *Disability & Society, 33*(6), 985–989. https://doi.org/10.1080/09687599.2018.1455627

Brown, N., Thompson, P., & Leigh, J. S. (2018). Making academia more accessible. *Journal of Perspectives in Applied Academic Practice, 6*(2), 82–90. https://doi.org/10.14297/jpaap.v6i2.348

Brownell, C. (2018, May 17). Canadian university professors spend roughly half their time on teaching. *Maclean's.* https://macleans.ca/education/canadian-university-professors-spend-equal-amounts-of-time-on-teaching-and-non-teaching-work/.

Clare, E. (2015). *Exile and pride: Disability, queerness, and liberation.* Duke University Press.

Ellis, C. S., & Bochner, A. P. (2006). Analyzing analytic autoethnography: An autopsy. *Journal of Contemporary Ethnography, 35*(4), 429–449. https://doi.org/10.1177/0891241606286979

Hamraie, A. (2016). Beyond accommodation: Disability, feminist philosophy, and the design of everyday academic life. *PhiloSOPHIA, 6*(2), 259–271. https://doi.org/10.1353/phi.2016.0022

Holman Jones, S. L., Ellis, C., & Adams, T. E. (2013). *Handbook of autoethnography.* Left Coast Press, Inc.

Kafer, A. (2013). *Feminist, queer, crip.* Indiana University Press.

Mellifont, D. (2023). Ableist ivory towers: A narrative review informing about the lived experiences of neurodivergent staff in contemporary higher education. *Disability & Society*, *38*(5), 865–886. https://doi.org/10.1080/09687599.2021.1965547

O'Donovan, M. M. (2010). Cognitive diversity in the global academy: Why the voices of persons with cognitive disabilities are vital to intellectual diversity. *Journal of Academic Ethics*, *8*(3), 171–185. https://doi.org/10.1007/s10805-010-9116-x

Price, M., Salzer, M. S., O'Shea, A., & Kerschbaum, S. L. (2017). Disclosure of mental disability by college and university faculty: The negotiation of accommodations, supports, and barriers. *Disability Studies Quarterly*, *37*(2). https://doi.org/10.18061/dsq.v37i2.5487

Shahjahan, R. A. (2015). Being "lazy" and slowing down: Toward decolonizing time, our body, and pedagogy. *Educational Philosophy and Theory*, *47*(5), 488–501. https://doi.org/10.1080/00131857.2014.880645

Walford, G. (2021). What is worthwhile auto-ethnography? Research in the age of the selfie. *Ethnography and Education*, *16*(1), 31–43. https://doi.org/10.1080/17457823.2020.1716263

Wigg-Stevenson, N. (2017). You don't look like a Baptist minister: An autoethnographic retrieval of 'women's experience' as an analytic category for feminist theology. *Feminist Theology*, *25*(2), 182–197. https://doi.org/10.1177/0966735016673261

Disability and Youth Ministry: The Book I'm Not Going to Write

Benjamin T. Conner

ABSTRACT

Since Amplifying Our Witness: Giving Voice to Adolescents with Developmental Disabilities *was published in 2012, little else has been written on disability and youth ministry. This article reflects on the ministry behind the book eleven years later, considers some of the important changes in the landscape of youth culture and disability in that time period, and calls for resources that address this reality written by scholars/practitioners who share life with disabled youth, are themselves disabled, and preferably both.*

This morning, I had the privilege of leading a discussion with Dr. Kirsty Jones and her disability and ministry class. Dr. Jones is a newly minted PhD from Georgetown University and coordinator of the Certificate in Disability Ministry at United Theological Seminary.[1] This was the second time in two years that I had the opportunity to meet with the group *via* Zoom—the first session on *Disabling Mission, Enabling Witness* (Conner, 2017) and this morning's session was a discussion generated by a podcast from when my wife, Melissa, and I joined the team at *The Two Cities— Theology, Culture, Discipleship* podcast. One student requested a bit more in-depth analysis of one of the stories I told in the podcast—one I have shared in various settings, innumerable times over the years about how a young man with cerebral palsy and an intellectual disability provided comfort and peace to his peer when I was unable to do so, despite my training and experience.[2] As I was speaking to the group and processing aloud my experience of that situation, it occurred to me that one thing that had changed in our relationship (the one between me and the youth to whom I was ostensibly ministering) was the power dynamics. This was the first time in this ministry that I felt helpless or powerless. In this moment, for the first time in my consciousness (though obviously it had always been true) I needed my friend Craig. I needed his presence. I needed him to minister to Bo and I needed him to minister to me. That experience changed everything for me—my theology of disability, my understanding of spiritual gifts, my expectations of Craig, my attentiveness to the work of the Holy Spirit around me, the way I organized our meetings together, and my understanding of discipleship. *Amplifying Our Witness*, published in 2012, was my way of articulating the theology and practice of faith that emerged out of my friendships and shared life with adolescents with intellectual and developmental disabilities and their families. As I was sharing this experience and reflecting on it, I felt gravity of the fact that that experience was 17 years ago, and I have not shared life with disabled youth in this deep way for over ten years!

To summarize, in *Amplifying Our Witness* my proposal was that ministry leaders should adopt a practice-centered approach in youth ministry, specifically with disabled youth. Written for a general audience, but still with an unwelcomed sheen of doctoral haughtiness, I offered the following theses which expounded my proposal:

1. One faithful and effective way to minister to and with adolescents and adolescents with developmental disabilities is to create spaces through practice-centered ministry in which durable friendships can develop.
2. When it comes to bearing witness to God's ongoing redemptive work in the world, nobody is impaired and they should not be disabled.
3. Developing a proclamatory program (our program includes all of our activities over the course of the year that support the ministry) will help us to be more effective in reaching our friends with developmental disabilities and will increase our capacity to communicate the Gospel more holistically. (Conner, 2012, pp. 3-4)

I still find this proposal compelling today, though now I would add more mutuality-language in my articulation of these theses. This way of sharing life with disabled youth, which I promoted as a way of discipleship and witness in the book and attempted to live out, has been affirmed as faithful by the responses of parents, youth, and volunteers and by the continuing community that persists today, even if that community has taken different forms. I still stay in touch with many of these young adults through social media and FaceTime from a distance while I teach and direct the Center for Disability and Ministry at Western Theological Seminary and I make sure to connect with some of them whenever I return to town. Ministry structures and organizations may come and go, but relationships endure. I have continued to grow up with these young adults, and they have continued to grow together over the past ten years in my physical absence, though not in an ecclesial setting. They have deepened their relationships through a day program at The Arc (which is run by two of the mothers who were highly invested in our youth group).[3] I visited several of these young adults at their Arc recently and was unreservedly greeted. Unreservedly—one of the things I appreciated the most about our years spent together. For seven years we had prayed together, engaged scripture together, practiced friendship, forgiveness, and hospitality together, always unreservedly.

In correspondence from a mother whose son, Sean,[4] was in our youth group years ago, a letter which is folded and tucked between the pages of my copy of *Amplifying Our Witness*, she described the period of time just after when her son first attended one of our gatherings.

> Sean had connected to one kid in particular so they got together outside of [the group meetings]. They did normal kid things, they ran around outside, played video games, and maybe watched a movie, on the surface nothing particularly special. That evening when Sean went to bed, he had the biggest grin I had ever seen, and told me that it had been the best day EVER! I told him I was so glad the that he had fun with his friend Matt. That was when Sean's eyes light up even more and he said, **"Wow, so this is what it feels like to have a friend?"** I will never forget the look on his face; it was pure joy. You see Sean had never had a friend before, something the rest of us probably took for granted as part of childhood. Having that feeling for the first time has changed Sean's life forever. There is tremendous sadness in seeing your child passed over, never invited to join in the fun just because he has a disability, but the joy in knowing that he has even one real friend takes away all that pain.[5]

She continued to explain that now, because her son has found a place of belonging, she also has a community of friends, having not pursued social interaction or been invited to another's house in over eight years due to the challenges of raising her son.

Where are these young adults 10 years later? Largely in the same space—living with their parents, dependent upon SSI benefits, involved in the community as volunteers, engaged in Special Olympics. Two of my friends who are on the autism spectrum have found fulfilling jobs: one doing laundry at a local hospital where his attention to detail is appreciated and one at a theme park and at *Ripley's Believe it or Not!*, where his overwhelming knowledge of all items within the building is coveted rather than met with sneers and disparaging comments. Another friend, Craig, volunteers at the Humane Society where his gentle presence is appreciated by the animals there. The fact that these three have been able to live into a vocation where their gifts and dispositions are valued is satisfying, but what gives me the most joy was that most of the youth with whom I shared seven years of my life have enduring friendships. But, I don't have these kinds of relationships with young people with disabilities anymore.

I'm not in touch daily with the struggles of parents. I'm not moving alongside disabled youth at a pace that would allow me to know them in any meaningful way. I'm no longer alongside them place-sharing (*Stellvertretung*) (Root, 2007, pp. 126–9) experiencing their joy and pain, possibilities and limitations, praises and laments, advocating on their behalf, and amplifying our shared witness. A book on youth ministry and disability simply can't be written at an academic distance from the lives of disabled youth. I don't know when it happened, but somehow ten years have passed. While I still have relationships with many of those persons who made up our youth group, we now live five states and a 12-h drive apart. Still, Craig and Patrick make sure I'm aware of the scores of the latest Virginia Tech sporting events (which was welcomed this year because of an historic women's basketball season) and Elizabeth gives me a hard time on social media anytime UVA bests the Hokies in any arena of competition. Sam keeps me updated on his latest job accomplishment or girlfriend. Alexis makes sure I'm tracking the marriages and children of her family as well as those of the volunteers who used to help with the youth group. Most of them, while they experience community, are still longing for intimacy—almost all missed the markers of homecoming and prom dates, boyfriends and girlfriends, they want to be married, they delight in their roles as aunts and uncles, yet with a dissatisfied longing to be a parent. Their parents are still anxious about what will become of them when they pass—where will they live? Who will support them? Unlike those young people in typical youth ministry, my friends haven't "aged out" though they are no longer welcomed because they are too old, and they are not finding a home in "age-appropriate" ministries. I had not foreseen this issue.

Perhaps the time is right for a book on youth ministry and disability to be written. But I am not the one to write it. And I'm not sure it should be a monograph. And, if it is a monograph, it should certainly be written by or coauthored with a disabled pastor/theologian. I had been planning to write a revised and updated version of *Amplifying Our Witness* for the past couple of years. There is certainly a need for *something*, and I was excited to make another contribution. I had just reunited with some of those young friends mentioned above, most now in their 30s, who were essential to my writing *Amplifying Our Witness* and I was preparing to interview them in order to gain a longitudinal perspective on our shared ministry. I was motivated to write this book because it could be folded into a grant-funded project that will be addressing other important "missing voices" in youth ministry.[6] I was supported by two research assistants from my Hope College youth ministry class, Sam Buoscio who contacted churches with vital disability ministries to learn more from their theology and practice, and Megan Smith, who was getting me up-to-date on the mental health crisis among youth in the US. In fact, I was filling out the PQA (a proposal questionnaire) when I realized *Disability and Youth Ministry* is the book I am not going to write.

Since I wrote the poorly titled (from a search engine standpoint) *Amplifying Our Witness*, a lot has happened. More movies and television shows have featured disabled persons/youth in positive roles and as thick characters. COVID raised issues in the disability community about what true access and belonging are and provided avenues for digital natives to find leadership roles in the church, and this included many disabled people. It also sparked controversy about the desire to return to church as it was pre-COVID, which for many persons with disabilities meant a return to inaccessibility.[7] For youth, the challenge of navigating COVID along with decisions around schooling and masking have heightened our awareness of, and in some cases exacerbated, mental health challenges among youth. Consider also, from the standpoint of the mental health crisis, the impact of gun violence on children and youth, which has surpassed car accidents as the leading cause of death since 2020 for that demographic.[8] Whether disabled or typically developing, the idea of a "moratorium on adult responsibility" or a safe space where one can work out their identity does not accurately describe the academic settings of youth when administrators, teachers, youth and children must be trained regularly in active shooter drills. I will address mental health more below.

When I was researching and writing *Amplifying Our Witness* from 2008-11, one in 125 children/youth were diagnosed autistic, with many fewer females receiving the diagnosis. By the time it was published in 2012 that rate had increased to 1:88. By 2020, when I first started imagining updating my book, the rate had increased again to 1:54[9] and now, on the other side of 2022, the CDC has the autism diagnosis at 1:36 (still almost four times more commonly diagnosed in boys than girls).[10] Add to these changes that shifts in technology and growth of social media and networked individualism (Rainie & Wellman, 2012; Zirschky, 2015), and I quickly realized that I was out of my depth. I was neither embedded in the lives of disabled youth nor academically prepared to understand them today. There were further issues related to academic conversation partners.

When I started researching and writing on the topic of disability and theology in the mid-2000s, most of the prominent authors were able-bodied men (obviously, Nancy Eiesland's seminal work *The Disabled God* (1994) and fifteen years later Deb Creamer's *Disability and Christian Theology* (2009) were important, and written by women who claim disability, however, still most of the books on the subject were authored by able-bodied men).[11] I am pleased to see that some of the most impactful books on ministry lately have been written by people who claim disability; Amy Kenny, a disabled female scholar and Lamar Hardwick, an African American man who has adopted the moniker Autism Pastor.[12] Youth ministry awaits such a contribution.

I had hoped that as the perception of disability shifted in culture from being understood primarily as a deficit to being conceived as an unsurprising aspect of human diversity that there would not be the need for another book on disability and youth ministry, it would become part of the broader youth ministry discussion, or that another book would be written on the subject by a disabled scholar/practitioner. But in ten years, not only has there not been another monograph on youth ministry and disability (there is one edited volume which I will address directly below); the most popular works that address youth ministry barely if ever consider disabled youth. There is one other book, but I hesitate to include it because it is more of a handbook, John Barone's, *A Place for All: Ministry for Youth with Special Needs* (2008), which predated *Amplifying Our Witness* and served an important role for catechizing Catholic youth, but the resource lacks theological depth and basically maps special education onto Christian ministry. It is helpful in that it offers some valuable though dated information about disabilities, some tips for creating more inclusive spaces and curriculums (particularly chapter 6), and some training tools for volunteer leaders. The book does little to challenge the medical model of disability and, as the title suggests, is more about ministry to and with youth with disabilities than amplifying their gifts and contributions.

The most recent, significant publication is an edited volume, *Embodying Youth Ministry* (Ellis & Langford, 2020) which is essentially a special edition of an academic journal masquerading as a book, written by academics, that can be yours for $160.00 (I write this as a contributor to the volume!). Important issues like embracing otherness, the limits of the concept of adolescence, theological anthropology, reimagining disability theologically, and a call to develop an approach to ethics where disability is not exceptional are among the topics addressed in this book. What all have in common (less one article, not mine) is that they seem to be written from an antiseptic distance from the lives of disabled youth. While a wonderful collection of theological reflections, I'm not sure *Embodying Youth Ministry* would be of great help to the youth pastor.

Beyond books, there are some other resources available. Fuller Youth Institute offers some blogs that address the issue at a cursory theological level along with some practical tips and the topic has been broached at Princeton's Institute for Youth Ministry in some deep and meaningful ways.[13] Orange Ministry, particularly Orange Students, offers insights on how to "integrate students with special needs into your youth ministry," in a "5 Things" approach, an approach that highlights the dignity of individuals, focuses on relationships, but is not nearly capacious or theologically thick enough lead a ministry to welcome the gifts and leadership of disabled youth. If one searches long enough it is possible to find some blogs, podcasts, and other resources that could prove useful. One is much more likely to find resources that focus on faith development of and ministry to children and families. What is needed?

Voice, vocation, and mental health

Voice

While I am not going to write the next book or develop the next resource on youth ministry and disability, I do have hopes for it. As I mentioned above, I would like to see more written from the grounded, intersectional experience of disabled theologians and pastors. This is the issue of voice— who has the authority to speak on the subject and what perspectives need to be foregrounded. Almeda Wright (2017), an African American scholar at Yale, can write on the spiritual lives of African American youth and Ralph Watkins (2011), an African American scholar and Peachtree Professor of Evangelism at Columbia Theological Seminary, can analyze what prophetic word the youth who inhabit hip-hop culture might have for the church. A host of Latino/a scholars contributed to *Hispanic Young People and the Church's Pastoral Response* (Cervantes, 1994), and *Pathways to Hope and Faith among Hispanic Teens* (Johnson-Mondragon, 2007). These authors share in the experiences of the youth about whom they write and can write with authority, integrity, and depth. The voices of disabled pastors and scholars are being featured more prominently in resources on disability theology and ministry, but not in youth ministry.

What would it mean for someone on the Autism spectrum to write a youth ministry text? Joseph Straus argues that autism may appear as an obvious diagnostic category, but if autistic persons were to articulate their experience, they might describe themselves as "a social group with a distinctive, shared culture" (Straus, 2013, p. 462). They wouldn't view their neurodiversity pathologically but would, instead, describe themselves as offering important differences from the norm in terms of cognitive style and worldview. Digital culture and the disability rights movement have created the space necessary for autistic culture to emerge through connectivity and visibility. Autistic self-advocates are demanding that they be the interpreters of their lives and experiences, as Nancy Bagatell, director of the Division of Occupational Science and Occupational Therapy in the UNC School of Medicine, describes:

> Behaviors, such as repetitive movements and lack of eye contact, which are considered problematic in the biomedical paradigm, need to be understood as a difference, and not considered a behavior that needs to be changed. In this discourse, people with autism are considered worthy individuals in and of themselves, not people who need to be cured, altered, or isolated from the world. Autism is seen as a fundamental part of who they are, not just something they have; that is, if their autism were eliminated, they would not be the same person" (Bagatell, 2010, p. 38).

I'm very interested in seeing a youth ministry text written by someone who offers more attention to details than I, someone who unlike me can be obsessively single-minded and deeply focused, is a visual thinker, has different linguistic and communication skills than the typical academic, and who can see structures and patterns that aren't obvious to most. I can't imagine such a book—and that is the point. *I* can't imagine it. Disabled scholars and practitioners have an experiential, perspectival, and hermeneutical advantage on me.

Vocation

Through the writings of Kathleen Cahalan, my friendship and shared work with Jane Patterson, and the projects associated with the Collegeville Institute around the theme, I have come to believe that vocation is one of the most important topics to address alongside youth. This includes disabled youth, who are called by Christ, given gifts of the Spirit, and participate in a community of witness. There are some compelling works on vocation and youth like Katherine Turpin and Anne Carter Walker (2014), *Nurturing Different Dreams*, David White's (2013), *Dreamcare: A Theology of Youth, Spirit, and Vocation*, and Dori Baker and Joyce Ann Mercer's (2007), *Lives to Offer: Accompanying Youth on Their Vocational Quests*. These books on vocation are challenging, thoughtful, and extremely valuable for youth ministry and the church. At the same time, none of these important books considers the vocation of youth with disabilities. This is a loss on many levels because disabled youth can challenge concepts associated with vocation by reframing questions like: what is capacity? Is "capacity" a term equivalent to "ability" or "competency" or is it a concept that relates to being a capacious presence—one who creates spaces with her/his body/mind? How do we define flourishing? Do we do it in a way that filters out many of my friends with disabilities? In what ways have middle-class values driven our vision of vocation for youth? Is it enough to graduate a sober virgin who then attends college and becomes a good citizen? What if developmental delay is not delay—what if this is it in terms of cognitive and social functioning? Has developmentalism guided our understandings of vocation such that someone who is considered profoundly disabled and has little capacity for self-reflection or agency can't be imagined as having a vocation? The lived experience of disability can challenge communities of faith to reconsider their conception of vocation and can open it up for reformation in response to the mysterious and surprising work of the Holy Spirit in the lives of disabled youth.

Mental health

Finally, according to the *New York Times's The Daily* podcast, "In 2019, 13% of adolescents reported having a major depressive episode, a 60% increase from 2007."[14] For years I have depended on the groundbreaking work of JoAnn Leavey (2015), who took the youth experience of mental health challenges seriously and centrally in her writing and employed the phrase "the interrupted self" to describe that experience. "The label of mental illness," she explains, "becomes the defining point of the self in relation to the social world, including a person's external identity and image and internal emotional responses to the social realities of stigma, labeling, and subsequent social and functional losses. This leaves youth with a sense of existential struggle to find new meaning in life from a place of disadvantage" (p. 129). Her interviews with youth with mental health challenges found that social stigma and social losses were identified by youth as the most impactful consequences. In fact, according to the youth she interviewed, the social impact of mental illness is often more difficult to deal with than the "illness" itself. Young people describe being ostracized and pushed to the margins and lament that they don't have positive images of themselves from media or, more importantly, from peer groups. They find themselves victims of actions over which they have little or no control and, furthermore, a victim socially because they are held to account for those actions as if they were willful acts. All of this contributes to the experience of an "interrupted self"—interrupted academics, interrupted friendships and activities, interrupted self-evaluation—during a time in which young people are longing for a sense of identity that is embedded within a community of belonging. Under what conditions might the challenges of disordered thinking, disordered feeling, and disordered behavior not have such steep social consequences?

Fortunately, post-COVID, there have been some significant resources for youth leaders to address this challenge. Sarah Griffith Lund (2022), *Blessed Youth: Breaking the Silence about Mental Health with Children and Teens* and the research, including podcasts and blogs, from Springtide Research Institute that highlights the experiences of youth with mental health challenges, especially through their, *The Voices of Young People Podcast*[15] is of particular value to the youth worker trying to make sense of today's youth. It seems to me that such conversations will contribute to the destigmatization and normalization of the experience of disability among youth and in the church. I hope they will continue.

Concluding thought

Even if I were to catch up with the academic conversation around adolescence, youth, mental health, autism, identity formation, human development, and discipleship, two more significant issues remain for me, as I detailed above: this issue of voice and the fact that I don't currently spend time sharing life with disabled youth and their families. I will not write the next book on youth ministry and disability, but John Swinton,

Chair in Divinity and Religious Studies, University of Aberdeen, and I are developing a series that intends to address issues of practical theology and disability by amplifying the voices of disabled scholars and practitioners. Our contribution to the series, jointly authored, is being written under the working title *Missing Voices in Disability Theology* and will feature the theological reflections and accounts of people who use augmented speech, have less commonly encountered disabilities that haven't been engaged in disability theology, or who have found that disability has exacerbated the "purpose gap" (Reyes, 2021)[16] and has diminished their voice.[17] In writing this book with disabled partners, I am realizing in profound ways I am limited by the perspective granted to me by my body-mind. We would welcome a monograph or edited volume on disability and youth ministry written by disabled scholar/practitioners.

Is it your turn?

Notes

1. An important program, one of two of its kind in the US, that is, sadly, not taking any more registrants.
2. Find a version of it in the introduction to *Practicing Witness: A Missional Vision of Christian Practices* (Grand Rapids: Eerdmans, 2011) or listen to my conversation with the wonderful hosts of The Two Cities podcast at http://www.thetwocities.com/
3. This national organization has many local chapters. Their mission is, "Promoting and protecting the human rights of people with intellectual and developmental disabilities and actively supporting their full inclusion and participation in the community throughout their lifetimes," https://thearc.org/
4. Not his actual name.
5. Personal correspondence, 2010, date not recorded.
6. See the important work being done by *The Missing Voices Project* at Flagler College led by Justin Forbes, https://missingvoices.flagler.edu/
7. See the opinion piece by Tish Warren Harrision, "Why Churches Should Drop Their Online Services" New York Times, January 30, 2022 https://www.nytimes.com/2022/01/30/opinion/church-online-services-covid.html, and the backlash on Twitter and beyond.
8. https://www.cnn.com/2023/03/29/health/us-children-gun-deaths-dg/index.html, accessed April 20, 2023.
9. https://www.autismspeaks.org/press-release/cdc-estimate-autism-prevalence-increases-nearly-10-percent-1-54-children-us, accessed April 13, 2023.
10. https://www.cdc.gov/ncbddd/autism/data.html, accessed April 13, 2023.
11. The disability and theology corpus included works by Jean Vanier, Henri Nouwen, Han Reinders, Tom Reynolds, John Swinton, Brian Brock, Bill Gaventa, Brett Webb-Mitchell (early on), Stanley Hauerwas (using disability as a means to think through ethics) and others. Biblical studies always seemed to have women more prominently involved.
12. Amy Kenny, *My Body is Not a Prayer Request: Disability Justice in the Church* (Grand Rapids: Brazos Press, 2022); Lamar Hardwick, *Disability and the Church: A Vision for Diversity and Inclusion* (Downers Grove: IVP, 2021).

13. https://fulleryouthinstitute.org/blog/5-tips-to-rethink-the-strengths-and-gifts-of-youth-with-disabilities, accessed April 13, 2023. For an example of Princeton Theological Seminary's offerings, listen to "A Vision for Disability and Ministry" from the *The Distillery* podcast, https://www.ptsem.edu/news/a-vision-for-disability-and-ministry and engage the material from the Disability & Faith Forum, https://disabilityandfaith.org/princeton-disability-and-youth-ministry-conference-reflections/
14. "Inside the Adolescent Mental Health Crisis: Young people in the Unites States are facing a new set of risks. What has the situation caught so many people off guard?" https://www.nytimes.com/2022/08/30/podcasts/the-daily/teens-mental-health-crisis.html, accessed April 14, 2023.
15. https://www.springtideresearch.org/community/podcast, accessed April 15, 2023. See also, *The State of Religion & Young People: What Faith Leaders Need to Know* (Springtide Research Institute, 2022).
16. The purpose gap is, in short, the gap between one's internal sense of calling or vocation and the external barriers to flourishing. While Reyes is addressing the purpose gap in relation to race, his arguments and insights apply equally well to those persons who experience a purpose gap due to ableism. Reyes posits, if "vocation is the call to life, then I claim here that external conditions have as much to do with one finding one's purpose as does one's internal discernment" (Reyes, 22). There is no way to talk about vocation and disability without addressing the larger social, academic, and ecclesial environment that pushes against flourishing and purpose.
17. The books in the series will be co-branded Intervarsity Academic and Western Theological Seminary's Center for Disability and Ministry, *Center for Disability and Ministry Books*. The first book slated to be published fall 2023 is *Disabling Leadership: A Practical Theology for the Broken Body of Christ* written collectively by Andrew Draper, Jody Michele, and Andrea Mae, all of whom are either disabled, have disabled children, or both.

Disclosure statement

No potential conflict of interest was reported by the author.

References

Bagatell, N. (2010). From cure to community: Transforming notions of autism. *Ethos*, 38(1), 33–55. https://doi.org/10.1111/j.1548-1352.2009.01080.x
Baker, D. G., & Mercer, J. A. (2007). *Lives to offer: Accompanying youth on their vocational quests*. Pilgrim Press.
Barone, J. E. (2008). *A place for all: Ministry for youth with special needs*. St. Mary's Press.
Cervantes, C. M. (Ed.). (1994). *Hispanic young people and the church's pastoral response. Prophets of Hope* (Vol. 1). Saint Mary's Press.
Conner, B. T. (2012). *Amplifying our witness: Giving voice to adolescents with developmental disabilities*. Eerdmans.
Conner, B. T. (2017). *Disabling mission, enabling witness: Exploring missiology through disability studies*. IVP Academic.
Creamer, D. B. (2009). *Disability and Christian theology: Embodied limits and constructive possibilities*. Oxford University Press.

Eiesland, N. L. (1994). *The disabled God: Toward a liberatory theology of disability.* Abingdon Press.

Ellis, W. W. and M. D. Langford, eds. (2020). *Embodying Youth Ministry: Exploring Youth Ministry and Disability.* Routledge.

Johnson-Mondragon, K. ed. (2007). *Pathways to hope and faith among Hispanic teens.* Instituto Fe y Vida.

Leavey, J. E. (2015). *Living recovery: Youth speak out on "owning" mental illness.* Wilfrid Laurier University Press.

Lund, S. G. (2022). *Blessed youth: Breaking the silence about mental health with children and teens.* Chalice Press.

Rainie, L., & Wellman, B. (2012). *Networked: The new social operating system.* MIT Press.

Reyes, P. B. (2021). *The purpose gap: Empowering communities ofcColor to find meaning and thrive.* Westminster John Knox Press.

Root, A. (2007). *Revisiting relational youth ministry: From a strategy of influence to a theology of incarnation.* IVP.

Straus, J. N. (2013). Autism as culture. In L. J. Davis (Ed.) *The disability studies reader* (4th ed., pp. 460–485). Routledge.

Turpin, K., & Walker, A. C. (2014). *Nurturing different dreams: Youth ministry across lines of difference.* Pickwick Publications.

Watkins, R. B. (2011). *Hip-Hop redemption: Finding God in the rhythm and the rhyme.* Baker Academic.

David, F., & White, D. F. (2013). *Dreamcare: A theology of youth, spirit, and vocation.* Cascade Books.

Wright, A. M. (2017). *The spiritual lives of young African Americans.* Oxford University Press.

Zirschky, A. (2015). *Beyond the screen: Youth ministry for the connected but alone generation.* Abingdon Press.

Index

For Product Safety Concerns and Information please contact our EU
representative GPSR@taylorandfrancis.com
Taylor & Francis Verlag GmbH, Kaufingerstraße 24, 80331 München, Germany

www.ingramcontent.com/pod-product-compliance
Ingram Content Group UK Ltd.
Pitfield, Milton Keynes, MK11 3LW, UK
UKHW051504141025
463795UK00028B/143